BIGGER THAN JUSSIE

THE DISTURBING NEED FOR A MODERN-DAY LYNCHING

OLA AND BOLA OSUNDAIRO

WORDS MATTER
P U B L I S H I N G
OUR WORDS CHANGE THE WORLD

Words Matter Publishing
P.O. Box 1190
Decatur, IL 62525
www.wordsmatterpublishing.com

ISBN: 978-1-958000-61-8
Library of Congress Catalog Card Number: 2023940209

TABLE OF CONTENTS

Table of Contents

INTRODUCTION

Every production requires a specific cast handpicked by directors and producers for the success of the production. The cast in this event was unequivocally selected. What is unknown are the identities of the producers and directors.

With that in mind, we gently remind the reader of the events happening in the U.S. at the time of the Jussie Smollett modern-day lynching hoax.

- For over 200 years, various anti-lynching bills had been brought before the House and the Senate. They never passed.
- December 2018: The revised anti-lynching bill went before the Senate once again. Passed. The House was not interested. The bill dies, again.
- January 29, 2019: Jussie arranged a modern-day lynching hoax in Chicago in the middle of a winter vortex, by two 'southern white men' screaming MAGA and racial and political slurs at him.
- Prominent people send supportive Tweets to Jussie, the words 'modern-day lynching' are mentioned in several prominent tweets.

- Sixteen days later the anti-lynching law is back, another revised version, passes the Senate unanimously. Two prominent Senators mention a modern-day lynching of a young black actor in Chicago when speaking of this bill. This time, **after** the Smollett lynching hoax the House immediately picks up the bill. The House has one holdout this time, that asks for the language of some of the bill to be revised. Once done, the House passes the bill with a revised name of The Emmett Till, bill.
- After 200 tries. After a modern-day lynching hoax. The U.S. finally has an anti-lynching law! So was the Smollett hoax *Bigger Than Jussie?*

Prologue

I'VE GOT A FUNNY FEELING

"You're under arrest!" the detective said as he showed me his Chicago Police Department badge.

Ola: Boarding the plane in Nigeria with my brother, I had an uneasy feeling. I mentioned it to my brother, Bola. He had a similar feeling. The moment the plane landed at Chicago O'Hare Airport; the feeling of unease returned. As I neared the plane door, I saw an agent checking passports. They never did that. Was this what I thought it was?

I stepped up to the customs agent and handed him my passport. The moment he saw my name, I saw recognition in his eyes. That was when I knew without a doubt he'd been looking for me...me and my brother!

Another customs agent stepped forward, "Come with me."

Reluctantly, I followed him to get my bags before he led me to a room where he searched my bags. I could tell by the way he barcly glanced at my belongings he was stalling. The question was, why?

Where was my brother? We hadn't been seated together on the plane. The last I saw him was when we boarded the plane. Where was he? I glanced as quickly as I could around the airport. He was nowhere to be seen. Had customs detained him as well? I was targeted; I knew that without a doubt. Was my brother targeted too? Once more, I looked around, hoping to see him.

The police were waiting as soon as I walked out of customs. "Give me your phone," the detective held out his hand.

I looked at his outstretched hand. He wanted my phone, but which one? I had three phones. Two were mine, and one was my mother's that she had sent home with me as it didn't work in Nigeria. If I asked for him to specify, he would no doubt want all three. Being difficult wouldn't help the situation. What choice did I have? I went to hand him my phone, and he told me to open it for him. I had no reason not to. I had nothing to hide.

After my rights were read to me, I asked for a lawyer. The detectives said nothing else to me. I didn't even know why I was detained. I had an idea, but the detective never said why. He just read me my rights and clammed up after I uttered the word lawyer.

As I handed over my now unlocked phones, my thoughts jumped to my girlfriend. It was the day before Valentine's Day. After two weeks in Nigeria, she would be angry if I missed the day! I didn't even have flowers or candy for her. I'd planned on surprising her, but this wasn't the kind of surprise I intended.

Bola: Like Ola, I'd had a bad feeling in Nigeria. I told my brother I thought they would be waiting for us when we arrived in Chicago. The news of the attack was on TV in Nigeria. People were posting about it on Twitter. The police were looking for two suspects. I felt that the police had an idea of who the suspects were, and it wasn't two racist white men. Maybe I was being paranoid, but I couldn't shake the feeling.

When I got off the plane, I had no idea where my brother was. I wasn't worried, as we had flown this way many times. We would meet up once we got through customs. I did a quick glance at the faces around me. I didn't see Ola anywhere. What I did see were the customs agents checking passports. For a moment, I stopped. Customs agents hadn't done that before. My brother and I had flown many times, and not once had I seen customs do that. It could be a new policy, but that feeling I had on the plane told me it wasn't.

Had my brother gone through customs? My brother and I hadn't done anything to be worried about. I wasn't concerned about that. I knew something could be made from nothing. I was no doubt over-thinking it. Not one to back down for any reason, I took a deep breath and stepped up to the customs agent. I smiled as I offered him my passport. I kept my smile in place as I watched him look at my passport, he then looked at another agent nearby. I thought about cracking a joke about my profile picture on my passport but decided not to push my luck at the moment.

The other agent took my passport and instructed me to follow him to the baggage claim. He waited while I got my luggage and a painting of Fela Kuti, a great musician and political figure from Nigeria I'd brought with me. The customs agent took me to a nearby area, where he thoroughly inspected my luggage before telling me I was free to go. There was something that didn't sit well with me about the whole thing.

I wasn't surprised when I stepped out the door with my bags and detectives were waiting. I was shown a badge and told they were Chicago Police to follow them and ushered me into a room. The customs agent went out as we came in. That room got a lot smaller over the next hour and a half.

I was instructed that the police had questions for me. I had questions myself. Where was my brother? Why was I being detained? I had done nothing wrong; what right did they have to hold me? As you can imagine, I didn't get answers to my questions, and they didn't get any to theirs.

I may have been a little confrontational, but they remained nice, almost friendly. After what seemed like forever, we left the room. They waited until I was outside to handcuff me and tell me my rights. I asked what the charges were but wasn't told. Where was Ola? Had they gotten him too? As I was loaded into the police car, I once more searched for my brother. Where was he?

Chapter One

ALLOW ME TO INTRODUCE MYSELF

Ola: Most people think I was born in Nigeria because of my heritage. I am an American, born to immigrant parents. I was actually born in 1991 on the north side of Chicago in Wrigleyville at St. Joseph's Hospital. I was the second son of three boys in a family of five children. I was named Olabinjo after my great-great grandpa. My name means 'birth to more wealth that resembles me.' My grandfather on my father's side gave me that name.

My mother was working at *Montgomery Ward* at the time. My father owned a clothing store. We were just your normal middle-class family. We weren't rich, but we weren't struggling or hungry either. My dad came from an influential Nigerian family. Not only did my grandfather own a hotel in Nigeria, but he was also a member of the secret service there too.

My earliest memory is of the 1993 NBA Basketball Championship Parade in Chicago. I was two years old at the time, but I remember being on my dad's shoulders watching the parade. Michael Jordan had led the Chicago Bulls to a third straight championship. This was the year Jordan decided he was done being a basketball player. The parade was held in celebration of the win. I don't know how I remember that considering I was only two, but I distinctly remember being there on my dad's shoulders. That is my favorite memory of my childhood.

When I was a baby, my parents went to Nigeria, but I have no recollection of that visit. I remember being six when my grandparents came to visit for the first time in Chicago. This was the first time meeting them, that I remember. My Grandmother made us eat cereal with water once. She wanted to teach us not to take things for granted and humble us. We had no choice but to eat it. I think it was *Cheerios*. But it could have been any cereal, and it would have been just as bad! It was disgusting! The visit was great, except for that. That was the nastiest thing! Thankfully she didn't make us do that ever again.

I attended a private school for kindergarten, Christopher House, and then transferred to a public school because of expenses. I was in public school from first through third grade; then, we moved to the Southside in 1999. My parents bought a four-unit apartment building. We stayed in one of the apartments while they rented out the other three. This was the first time my brother and I started going to the same school together. A stronger bond between Bola and I began to form then.

There was a time when I was five or six years old; I was lying on the floor watching TV when Bola came and dropped a heavy computer keyboard on my head. To this day, I don't know what the reason was. He never did get punished for that. I asked him if he remembered why he did it, but he didn't. He was only two or three. There wasn't a lasting impression, so it must not have hurt too much.

There was a time around six when I got really sick. I don't know what I had, but the doctors said it was serious. They said I needed surgery. The doctors were adamant I needed surgery, or I wouldn't get better. My grandparents and parents were just as adamant that I wouldn't be having the surgery! My family prayed over me, my parents prayed at my side, and my grandparents from Nigeria did it over the phone and asked for healing. Whatever was making me sick disappeared. The Almighty knew how to heal me! This was just one incident of how faith has touched my life. Maybe it was a miracle, but prayer really did save me.

In 2001, I was in the fifth grade. That was the year I had my first girlfriend, Herminia. Sadly, she was not the reason I remember my fifth-grade days. I remember them because that is where I was when that horrible act of terrorism happened on September 11, 2001. That horrifying event is one of those things in life that you remember where you were when you heard about it. Like when Malcolm X or Martin Luther King Jr. died. Or Elvis and Marilyn Monroe. You can ask any older person, and I bet they could tell you exactly where they were when they learned of the loss of any of those people I mentioned.

Ask my generation, and they will be able to tell you where they were when word of that first plane hit the North Tower. Some of us might have actually seen the second plane hit the south tower on TV while watching coverage of the first. Planes were grounded for the first time across the USA, and there were tons of speculation that more planes were targeted. No one knew when it would end, but the sights on television and the reporter's expressions and tone told you that this was serious, and they were all scared. As a frequent flier of long flights, this gave me a moment of concern.

From elementary school up to sixth grade, I was bullied. In sixth grade, I got into my first fight with this white kid, Eddie. I was picked on for being African and darker-skinned. I was bullied by gang members but not in a way like they were trying to recruit me. They were just being bullies.

This was my first run-in with the law. I took a knife to school; this was back before school violence was as bad as it is now. I don't know that I really thought it through taking the knife to school; I was just eleven. Would I have used it? No. It was really a stupid thing to do. I guess maybe I felt better having it with me. Like the thought that I had it for protection, yet I wouldn't have actually used it, so I don't know. Looking back, I can think of all kinds of reasons why I wouldn't have used it. Hindsight is 20/20.

Anyway, another student saw the knife and reported it to one of the teachers. I had already gotten rid of it, which shows I never had any intention of using it on anyone. Once the teachers confronted me about it, I could have said no, I don't have anything, and they would never have found it. I don't know; I guess I was a naive kid. I showed them where I had stashed it. They ended up calling the police, who put me in handcuffs. My mom was called. I remember her crying. They hauled me away to jail. I don't remember exactly what happened after that.

I wasn't charged for anything, but I was taken away in handcuffs. That was a big ordeal. This was just two years after Columbine. At the time, everyone was aware of school shootings, but I never thought it would happen at my school. The thought didn't cross my mind when I took that knife to school that it could be construed as me planning to harm someone in this manner.

With the continual school shootings, if I were to have been in school in these difficult times, I wouldn't have just been arrested and let go. I would be serving time, even though I had no intention of using it. I am thankful my school days are over, but fearful for those children who still could face something horrific. Who knew that sending your children to school to learn would put them in fear for their lives, hiding under desks, in cabinets, and in bathrooms, with teachers locking their doors to protect them from armed gunmen who are also children?

Taking that knife to school was a stupid idea, but at the time, I didn't know what else to do. I should have talked about the bullying with an adult. I thought I could handle it, though the knife wasn't the reason I felt that way. As I have said, I wouldn't have used it. At that age, I thought I was big and bad. I could handle things myself.

Back in those days, though it wasn't that far back, bullying at school wasn't as horrible as it is now. The children of today must deal with so much more than I did. I was a nineties baby and grew up in the 2000s, but cyberbullying is now something that is out of control! I don't remember ever having an issue with that in school. Back then, the bullies preferred to be face-to-face with you. That enabled you to fight back if you wanted, with fists, not words. Bullying today is done from the safety of a computer screen or cell phone by people who talk big and bad but are actually petty and scared.

I got whooped for taking that knife to school. My mother was the one who enforced punishment growing up. My dad only put his hands on me a few times growing up. If he whooped us, we had done something extreme. Unlike my mother, my father is a big figure; his stature and his voice tend to give off the impression not to approach him. I wouldn't say I was terrified of him, but I feared him because of his demeanor. You knew just from looking at him; he was a man you didn't want to push too far. I knew if he was talking, to listen.

I didn't need to be punished for taking that knife to school. Seeing my mother in tears was punishment enough. That image is still with me today. A constant reminder of how I hurt my mother with something I shouldn't have done. Something that, had I really thought it through, I would never have done.

I was an A and B student, with an occasional C. I had to go to summer school in the fourth grade because we transferred from Northside to Southside. We moved, and as a result, I ended up having to make up some time in summer school. It happens. But it really sucks to have to give up your summer because of a move your parents made.

I loved science. There is something about it that intrigued me. It is forever changing and growing the same way I am. I made a volcano once as a project. I know a lot of kids say that, but I liked to figure out what would make the volcano explode. I made sure when mine exploded, it created a booming sound, and then the lava flowed everywhere! Mine was by far the best, but I'm sure every kid thinks the same. I can't remember the grade I got on it, but I'm sure it was a good one.

When we were young, we collected *Pokémon* cards and *Yo-Gi-Oh* cards. We loved them. That was a big thing for us in our childhood. Just because our culture is Nigerian doesn't mean we liked different things kids our age in America liked; we are Americans, after all. Collecting those cards was fun! Some of them are worth major money. I wonder if I still have any?

Let me preface this by saying I wasn't a fat kid, but I loved sugar. I was also very independent. We went to old country buffet, and when we got home, I wanted some *Kool-Aid*. It was on the top shelf, so I had to get on the counter to get the *Kool-Aid*. I slipped and cut my head open on the deep freezer. My mom had to rush me to the hospital. I got six staples in my head. I learned not to climb after that.

The first time I got into trouble, I was seven or eight. I was at this camp, and there were rowboats. We had taken a few of them out on the lake. I wanted to show off like children do, so I jumped from one boat to the other. I didn't think it was a big deal, but everyone else did! I got in a lot of trouble and was kicked out of camp. I never went there again. Bola didn't get the chance to go. He probably wouldn't have been allowed if he wanted to, for fear he would do something like I did.

I didn't get into a lot of fights the way Bola did, but there was this one time when we were younger I fought with Bola. I don't even remember what we were fighting about. We're brothers; fighting is mandatory. I'm sure we fought more than this one time, but this one stands out. It was during our time on the Southside. We were fighting, and I pushed him through a window.

I didn't plan on that happening; it was just something that happened in the heat of the fight. He wasn't badly hurt, just a cut over his elbow. I was punished, of course. Winning that fight wasn't worth the pain I caused him or the pain my punishment caused me. When I was younger, I said I won the fight, as he ended up the one bleeding. Whoever draws first blood is the winner, right? I'm sure I remember hearing that at one point. I'm also sure Bola wouldn't agree.

It was around this time, when we were living in Southside, that I saw a newspaper article on an eleven-year-old Russian kid. He was a young bodybuilder. It just fascinated me. A boy around my age was doing something like that. I remember telling myself this is what I want to do in life. From then on, I started trying to figure out how to make that a reality. The people who had that kind of look were football players, so that is what I ended up getting into. I joined the Peewee football league in sixth or seventh grade.

My second run-in with the police happened when I was around eleven or twelve. My friend and I were walking down an alley when the police stopped us. We hadn't done a thing; they just stopped us. We were put in handcuffs. They didn't say why they were detaining us. One of them kneed me in the crotch. The other cop used his gun and hit my friend in his private parts. After they were done with us, they uncuffed us and let us go. I can't say with any certainty that this was the first time I saw police behaving as if they were above the law, but that was definitely what was going on. They thought they could detain us and do such things because of who they were. And people wonder why so many people distrust the police.

When we lived on the Northside, the police kicked down our door. It was a case of mistaken identity, but that didn't stop the police from arresting my father. They found bullets in the house but no gun. The police stole my father's FOID (Firearm Owners Identification Card), which is required by Illinois law for all gun owners. This card said my father was legally allowed to have a gun, even though, at that moment, he didn't have it in his possession.

Regardless of where it was, he was legally allowed to have it, but since it wasn't there, he was arrested. If not for that reason, I don't know what else it could have been. The police admitted to the mistaken identity, but they still arrested him! Because they found bullets and no gun! If they had found a gun with no bullets, what would they have used as a reason to arrest him? I wonder.

Before my father went to court, he had to get a new FOID card, as the police had taken his and not returned it. I think they said he didn't have one. An excuse they must have used for a legal reason to have arrested him! This shows how ridiculous this was, as there was no gun but bullets found!

The judge verified my father had a FOID card, then prayed for my father and dismissed the case. Just another reason we have to stay away from law enforcement.

Our parents made it a requirement that we take our sisters along if we wanted to go to our friend's party. While there, I witnessed a gang initiation. There was this gang, SWB—Southwest Boys—that had a ten-second violation; what that means is they had four or five members beat on potential members for ten seconds. As long as they take what is being done to them, they become a member. Not as bad as some gang's initiations, but not exactly easy either. The other gang members were allowed to beat on you as hard as they wanted in those ten seconds. The guy passed. I don't know why the initiation was happening at the party, but it was.

There was this one time when a friend of mine named Adrian, Bola, and I were walking home from school with my younger sister. We were walking and talking as kids do. For some reason, my sister was pretending like she was going to kiss Adrian. I don't remember if she even told us why. She didn't mean anything by it; it was just a joke.

Unfortunately, my father happened to be driving by right as my sister was in Adrian's face, playing like she was kissing. When we got home, out of nowhere, my father whooped us! Not my sister, who was the reason we were getting whooped, us, Bola, and I! He had seen her kiss, Adrian, even though she hadn't really, but Bola and I were the ones in trouble! He didn't even say anything to her about it!

Looking back, my brother and I got whooped a lot for things my sisters did. We had to clean the house and do whatever chores needed to be done too. As a result, I had a touch of animosity toward them. I loved them, but there was a little animosity.

We may not have gotten to Nigeria as often as we would have liked, but we did have family from Nigeria come to us. My dad's younger brother, Uncle Jimmy, visited; we tortured that man! One night when everyone was supposed to be sleeping, my older brother sent me and my younger brother, Bola, to knock on Uncle Jimmy's door. I should have known something was up when my older brother didn't do this himself. But he was the oldest, and we looked up to him. He had us do this two or three times!

The last time we went to do it, Uncle Jimmy was waiting around the corner. He had hidden when we were running back from the prior knock. As soon as we knocked on the door, he came around the corner to get us. We ran to our rooms. In my room, I hid under my bed. He tried to spank me while I was under the bed but couldn't quite reach me. Bola ran to our mother's room. I don't know if Uncle Jimmy got him or if my mother was the one who punished him. It must not have been a big to do, or I would surely remember it now.

Our parents were always taking us to parades or traveling to different countries. Not just to Nigeria but to Dublin, Amsterdam, and many others. I have great memories of discovering these countries and their cultures. We were always learning about others and finding ways to better ourselves. I loved Dublin, Ireland. There was just something about that place. My late aunt lived there. We looked forward to seeing her as much as we did Ireland.

Our family is very religious. We went to church every Sunday. Anytime there was an overnight vigil, we were there praying. Religion is a very large part of our childhood, going back to my grandfather.

When I was at home in Nigeria, I would play with my cousins. My grandmother had a shop where she sold food in front of the house. I'd eat or help her, sometimes both. It was a time I could just hang out with her. A time that I am thankful for now.

My grandfather spent his days at the hotel he owned. He wasn't physically working there; he was there to ensure everything was going as it should. On occasion, I would go with him. My grandfather didn't like driving. Sometimes, he'd have a driver. There was this one time when he was driving, and I was in the passenger seat. I fell asleep. My grandfather slapped me to wake me up. He said, "Am I your chauffeur? Am I your driver?" I learned not to fall asleep again. To some, that may sound harsh, but I didn't see it that way. He was teaching me respect.

Nigeria isn't like America. We have four regions, northern, southern, western, and eastern. Within these regions are thirty-six states under one federal capital territory. Ogun State is in the southwestern part of the state. Abeokuta is the capital and is known for a big rock that our ancestors called Olumo Rock.

Names in Nigeria, as in America, have meaning. Olumo is derived from two words. "Olu" means God/deity, and "mo" means molded. In the nineteenth century, this rock was used as a natural fortress during warfare between the tribes. My people, the Egba, lived there. The rock gave my people shelter.

The Oyo Empire was the main Yoruba, our ethnic group, and our tribe. They were the central figure of the empire. My people broke away from the Oyo, but we still speak the same language. By breaking away, we no longer paid tribute to them anymore. Because Olumo Rock gave us shelter, we were able to defeat the other tribes.

If you saw the rock today, you would see where my people slept, prepared, and cooked food. Our heritage is rich around this rock. There are caves that can be explored. There is this feeling that comes over me when I am there of family, of belonging, of royalty. This is but one of the stories of my ancestors that my grandfather has shared with me.

At Christmas, we would go to our grandfather's place in Lagos. We would spend lots of time there in the winter through New Year. I loved the time with my grandfather. I miss those days of hearing stories of my ancestors.

If Christmas fell on Sunday, we'd go to church twice. There were so many of us, with all the cousins, that my grandparents would take all of us in a bus. My grandparents loved having so many of us. I remember how much my grandmother loved me. She passed away in 2018 on August 12. She loved each one of us. She never showed bias to anyone. Each one of us knew she loved us and felt that every moment she was with us. I am thankful for every moment I had with my father's side of the family.

Unfortunately, I didn't know my grandparents on my mother's side. Her mother died in a car accident before I was born. She wasn't that close to him. When her mother died, he tried to claim some of her properties as his own. My mother had to fight him for that.

In 2005 I graduated middle school, and we moved to Nigeria. I thought we were just visiting. When I realized we were actually moving, I was very unhappy. My parents thought it was a good time for us to get closer to our family and learn about our culture. Looking back, I think it is one of the best things we ever did. At the time, all I wanted was to stay in America and attend high school with my friends.

Ola and Bola

Our grandparents

God's Grace, the family home

The hotel our family owns

Chapter Two

MY NAME IS...

Bola: To be honest, I don't know where I was born. I've never asked my parents, but I suppose it was in Chicago, like Ola. I know I was born in 1993, two years after Ola. I was born with water in my lungs. The technical term is Transient Tachypnea of a newborn. Basically, I had a mild respiratory problem that happened after birth and lasts about three days. Sort of like bronchitis, but not exactly. I spent a long time in the hospital. My mom took extra care of me. I think this is why I'm so close to her. My two sisters were born after me, making up the rest of us five children. When I was little, I loved milk. I would take the milk to my mother so she would give me some all the time. It earned me the nickname the Milkman.

As Ola said, we come from a very religious family. We were at church every Sunday, no matter what. We celebrated Thanksgiving at the church each year. This wasn't like family Thanksgiving. This is different with the church. We went to the Celestial Church of Christ, or CCC, which is a white garment church. That means everyone wears white and you don't wear shoes in the church. You take your shoes off at the entrance of the church. It is a very spiritual church that believes heavily in the Holy Spirit.

This is going to sound so messed up, but at the time, I was two or three years old and bored out of my mind, and I found a way to relieve the boredom. It wasn't that I didn't enjoy the sermons at church; it was that it was hard to sit in the same place for hours. Sometimes Church seemed to run a little long. I would find little ways to relieve my boredom by picking on those around me. At least on those who wouldn't tell on me. I was looking to relieve boredom and not get a whooping when I got home. There was this one thing I did, that I never admitted to, and probably shouldn't now. If there was a baby around me, I would wait until everyone had their eyes closed and I would pinch the baby and then close my eyes as if I was listening to the prayer.

The parents would try to calm the baby without speaking in the middle of the prayer. As soon as the baby stopped and the parent once more shut their eyes, I'd pinch it again. At the time, I was too young to really understand how that was wrong. I was just looking for a way to entertain myself.

The first school I remember going to was Christopher House in 1996 on the north side of Chicago. I wasn't there at the same time my brother was. I was three or four, but I remember. My favorite teacher, there was Robert. He was Hispanic. For a teacher, he was very cool.

Christopher House is where I first remember interacting with females. The first time I knew I liked women. She wasn't a woman; she was a girl the same age as me. I mean, I did like women too. I had some aunts that I liked. They weren't blood-related, just other moms in the neighborhood; they liked me too. Not like that, but you know.

Marissa was the first girl I remember messing with. The bathroom was a unisex restroom at Christopher House. Whenever the teacher would read us a story, I would ask to go to the restroom. She'd wait a few seconds, then ask if she could go. The teacher didn't suspect a thing. We were very slick at a young age. The things we did....

The most memorable thing that happened at Christopher House wasn't Marissa and our time in the unisex restroom; it was the day I was eating sausage for breakfast. I had taken a bite when suddenly my favorite teacher, the one I mentioned earlier, Robert, came up to me and sort of put his fingers on both sides of my mouth to make me spit it out. It was pork, something we didn't know at the time. We didn't eat pork. It's part of our religion; well, it's in the Bible. Leviticus 11:7 'And the swine, though he divides the hoof, and be cloven footed, yet he cheweth not the cud; he is unclean to you.' Many Christians don't follow it, though. That really stuck out in my head.

Growing up in Wrigleyville near Gill Park, we were surrounded by a diverse set people. There were a lot of Africans that stayed there. There was a mixture of families there, African and Nigerian, amongst others. My parents knew them all. We would do all kinds of things together. We went to the same church and schools. We had birthday parties where everyone in the neighborhood came to celebrate. We were one big family with different backgrounds.

We were very close with a family before we went to Nigeria. Their last name is Odedina. They were one of the only if not the only family that my parents let me or my siblings sleep over at their house. They did not let us sleep over at anybody else's house at all, even if we were very close to them. They had, I believe, five children, four girls, and one boy. I was really close to that boy. We still talk to this day. They used to throw the best parties. It was always fun. In many ways, the neighborhood felt like one big family.

I had many aunts, and mothers of other families, who we called aunts. When we were outside playing or riding our bikes, there was always a parent somewhere watching to make sure we were safe. More than once, we were babysat by one of the neighborhood mothers and vice versa. It was like some sort of unwritten agreement between them; we were able to run free as long as there was one of the aunts with an eye on us. I called the women aunts, even though they weren't blood-related. It was how we showed our respect.

I have always been a ladies' man. When it came to the aunts, they loved me. They would always call me their husband or boyfriend and whatnot. I was very likable amongst the older ladies. It was my charm. There were uncles as well, but we weren't as tight with them. My one favorite uncle at the time, Uncle Dean, would always play with us kids. We really appreciated him. He's still alive, but we aren't as close as we were. We do stay in contact with him, though. There are a number of aunts and uncles we are still in contact with. Family is family, even if you've moved on.

Whenever a child had a birthday, we would have a big party, and everyone in the neighborhood would come. I had so many aunts and uncles, and cousins living there. The blood-related kind and the love-related kind. I don't know why but every time my cousins and I got together, we would fight. Not really fighting, just a playful punch here or a playful punch there. It was a thing we did growing up. It gave us a kind of thrill. I guess that is why I like boxing now.

I always played rough with bigger kids. I don't know if it was because Ola is older and I was hanging with him, and as a result, I hung out with his friends, or if I just preferred to hang out with the older crowd. Even though some of those cousins were older than me, I still held my own in the fighting. I don't remember losing. Ola likes to say he beat me once when he shoved me through a glass window because I was bleeding. I disagree with that whole who drew blood first is the winner mentality.

After Christopher House, we moved to west lakeview. Wrigleyville is in Lakeview, but we moved a little more west than north, closer to Ravenswood, across the street from Lakeview High School. After Christopher House, I attended Walt Disney Magnet School.

A lot of people don't know Walt Disney was born in Chicago. There is a school named after him there, the Walt Disney Magnet School. A magnet school has an open space environment. The student body was made up of the surrounding neighborhoods. There are different races and cultures in every class. The teachers teach in a team-teaching format.

The school was just east of where we lived, sort of between Lakeview and Uptown, what is considered Chicago's lakefront. I went there only a year or two, but I remember going on field trips to museums and zoos. I loved going on field trips! I was fascinated with the places we went to. I have always liked learning new things; it helps me to grow as a person.

I was kind of a rebel back then; in a way, I still am. I like to do things my way—my way, or the highway. I would throw fits and act out a lot of the time. When I was at Walt Disney Magnet School, we went on this field trip to Dominick's Grocery. I don't know why we went on a field trip to Dominik's. Maybe it was to see the crabs they had in a box. I don't know why we would have, but anyway, things didn't go my way at one point. I was so mad! I kicked my shoe off because I was so upset. I got in trouble for that. I don't remember what kind of punishment I got, but the teachers had to do something.

Even though I was a rebel, the teachers still liked me. They didn't want to punish me for whatever trouble I was in because I was so likable. It would come down to how it would look to the other students if I got by with whatever I did. They couldn't let it slide with me and then punish someone else for doing the same thing. Once I had pushed them to their limit, they would reluctantly punish me in some way. My classmates liked me as well. I am just that kind of guy; everyone likes me. There wasn't a girl in the school I wasn't crushing on at some point. What can I say? I'm a ladies' man.

There was this one girl I was crushing on, Katie, and we were going on a field trip. I don't remember where, but her dad was one of the chaperones. I wouldn't say she was my girlfriend, but we were holding hands. To make sure her dad didn't see us, I put my jacket over our hands. I've been thinking about her lately and have tried to find her on social media. It would be nice to reminisce and see what she is up to.

I always wanted my mother or one of my parents, well really my mother, to be one of the chaperones. But it never happened. My mother was very busy. At the time, she worked for *Montgomery Ward* doing something with computers, I think. My dad owned a store and then did something in cyber security. The last thing he did before we went to Nigeria was drive an armored truck.

I guess the reason I liked the field trips was that my parents always took us places. Ola mentioned that. Like my brother, I loved Dublin. There is something about the land and the people of Ireland that makes it stand out, not to mention my aunt lived there.

Even though our parents were working, I never felt neglected. We were taught what we needed to know as we grew. We were given all the new Jordans when they came out, the new consoles, *PlayStation*, *Xbox*, *Game Boy*, *Nintendo 64*, you name it, we had it. We loved playing all the games that came out. *Pokémon*, of course, *Halo* and *Zelda* were just a few of our favorites. We played *NFL Blitz* and *Madden*, naturally.

Ola and I loved *The Lion King*. I loved the song, *Hakuna Matata*, much the way everyone did. Watching it and being taught our heritage made us the men we are today. It just resonated with me. One thing my parents instilled in me; is we were royalty. We are princes, kings. My mother's surname is Adeoye, which means our crown and her family is royalty. We were told at a young age we were princes. We were kings. We were never lacking.

As Ola mentioned, we moved to the southside in 1999. That is when I started going to Eberhart. I was in the first grade. This was the first time Ola and I were in the same school.

In 2000 we went to Nigeria to celebrate my grandfather's birthday. We met a lot of my cousins at the time. We were the older cousins, which meant the younger ones had to listen to us. It was his 70th birthday as he was born in 1930. That's when I saw a lot of the culture in Nigeria. There was this thing they did during the celebration; they sprayed money on him. That means placing money on the body of the celebrant. It is a tradition to do this at birthdays, weddings, most any celebration. It is to signify happiness and good fortune for that person.

He was dancing, and everyone would put money on him. I remember a day or two after we were at the house and in his room. There was a bed full of money, and I was thinking in my head, like, dang, we hit the lottery, and we're rich because there was a lot of money. It was like a pile, a big pile of money on there. Seeing that made me feel like we had a lot of money at the time.

I remember a song we used to sing back then. There was a little girl that they would bring that sang the same song every time. The song was very distinct because I still remember it to this day. It is customary to sing it at celebrations.

At that time in Nigeria, I was very protective of my mother, not just her, generally of the women around me, but especially my mother. I don't know why this particular visit affected me this way. When I saw my dad's friend dancing near my mother, I told him that I would smoke him if he didn't stop dancing with my mom. I was six or seven, but I told him I was going to smoke him if he didn't leave my mother alone. I'm not sure what I would have done if he hadn't stopped.

My parents tried to get me to use Yoruba, the language. I knew the language, but I couldn't really speak it. I understood some of it, the numbers; I understood a good bit, but to speak, it was a little difficult for us. Odedina's, though, had at that time never been to Nigeria. I'd been to Nigeria more than them, but they could speak the language really well.

There was this one time when Ola had a basketball tournament at Marquette Park when we lived on the Southside; he won the championship. They gave him a trophy. I remember being upset that I didn't get one. But I didn't play, therefore no trophy, but I still wanted one. I usually couldn't play sports with them because I was younger. The coach gave me a baseball pendant, and I was happy to receive it even though it wasn't a trophy.

I had a chip on my shoulder. I wanted to prove myself. After not getting a trophy, even though I got a pendant, I found myself wanting to prove to myself I could do better. I just needed to work hard and be given an opportunity. That's why in class, made me want to get to be the best that I could be to show people that I can do it!

My first-grade teacher, Ms. Holly, I really liked. I don't know what was wrong with me, but I was attracted to her. I was young and found my teachers were hot. There must have been something wrong with me. She was having a baby, but I thought she was still hot.

I remember first grade was the first time we did any kind of celebration for Saint Patrick's Day. Ms. Holly told us a story of how a little leprechaun stole the treasure, a bunch of little coins and turned the room upside down. We had to search the classroom and find the coins. That was a memorable moment from those days. I think it stands out because of how fun it was. Not to mention Ms. Holly was attractive.

Like my brother, science was my favorite subject. I enjoy the discovery of learning how things came to be. I was very interested in how our bodies operated and how viruses work. Possibly using the same mechanism virus use to replicate good cells in our body. With science, the reason why a volcano erupts could lead to being able to stop eruptions or give some form of warning so people could escape in time. With science, anything was possible.

I still use science in my day-to-day life. Did you know science can help with exercise and wellness?

On the Southside, was when we really had freedom from our parents. We were able to be out of sight without them freaking out. We spent time with an array of people each day. Our parents were working and were very occupied to be worried about if we would be safe while they were away. When we were in Northside, we had aunts and uncles that kept up with us.

We were older, so we were able to walk the two blocks to school. Looking back, I think the Southside was where I was happiest before moving to Nigeria. There was just so much freedom there, which is very important for a growing boy looking to explore the world around him.

Adrian, the friend Ola mentioned, was one of our friends we hung around with a lot. One time when we were hanging with him, we were curious about smoking. The kids we hung around with did, so naturally, we wanted to give it a go. We wanted to smoke something, but we didn't know what. You won't believe what we smoked! We took a piece of paper, and the only thing we had was a pencil. We shaved the pencil and tried to smoke the pencil shaving. I have no idea why we did that. There were so many kids in our school that were already smoking. Kids from first grade to eighth. These kids were already smoking weed. Though I had smoked it that one time. I never smoked weed. I think Ola did.

At this time, we were testing our entrepreneurial status. We were so smart! After the disaster with smoking pencil shavings, we decided to branch out. Literally! We took a branch and broke off the leaves on it. We put it in a baggie and sold it to some older Mexicans. That didn't go over well.

Ola: When I was a little older, I did experiment with weed. I never tried alcohol when I was young, but I did give weed a try. There was this time my brother and I were with some friends, I'm not sure how old we were, but we were riding around. I was smoking weed with my friends, but Bola didn't. Our friends dropped us back off at home. My brother and I were in the yard, and my dad happened to be outside. He was looking for us. I was high as hell, and my dumbass smelled like weed. Like an idiot, I walked by him, and he smelled it.

This was one of the three times that he whooped our asses. He tells us to go inside. My brother was smart, knowing what was going on. He hurries and rubs his hands on the grass so he doesn't smell anything like smoke. Once we got inside, my dad gave me hell. He smelled our hands. Mine smelled like weed; Bola's didn't. So, my dad made me take off my clothes and lay on the floor butt-ass naked! He started giving me the works. I didn't smoke again until much later in life.

Chapter Three

THERE GOES THE NEIGHBORHOOD

Bola: A lot of the people in our neighborhood were gang members. The Southside was where we really were introduced to gangs. The neighborhood was mostly Hispanic, but there were other cultures there too. The Latin gang was the Two-Six. The black gang were known as the Gangster Disciples. A lot of the young kids in my school were members of one of the gangs. We hung around with some of the kids who were in the gang. By doing so, we had their 'protection,' you could say. No one ever messed with us from either gang.

There was this guy, Brian, and I were super competitive. We weren't friends by any means. I used to get into a lot of fights. Not because I wanted to fight but because people around me wanted to fight me. I don't know why; maybe they were jealous or something. Maybe they were intimidated by me. I wouldn't start them, but I would defend myself! My thing was, if you were dumb enough to start a fight with me, you had better be ready for me to finish it!

Of course, I won every fight, but Brian kept trying! Poor guy! He should have given up; he was never going to beat me. We would fight any time we passed each other. On the weekend, we would ride our bikes, and if we saw each other, we would get off our bikes and start boxing. Then we would get back on our bikes and ride away. I don't know if it was some type of animalistic stuff or what, but we did it every time.

At one point, we became some sort of friends because we were going to form a two-man group. Can two people be considered a group? Maybe we were more like a duo. Whatever it was, it didn't happen. It was right before we moved to Nigeria, so the group or duo broke up though I'm not very sure the group broke up as it was never officially started. I don't remember what the group was even supposed to be about.

I have to say; when we were living on the Southside, I was the happiest before we went to Nigeria. We had more freedom there; that freedom was key. But my favorite school was in the Northside. I remember so many things from my school years, but I have the fondest memories at Christopher House and my favorite teacher, Robert. My grades were good no matter what school I was in. I was mostly an A student. Maybe it was my favorite school because that unisex bathroom had something to do with it.

We weren't allowed to have a pet until we moved to the Southside. We had a huge yard. Our first pet was Leslie; she was a cream-colored dog. She was a smart dog, a very smart dog. She was short, but she was able to jump the fence. She did so often, mostly when we weren't there. Then she would jump back over. She wouldn't use the bathroom in the yard; she would jump over the fence, and then once she was done, she jumped back in the yard, which was actually a good thing! We didn't have her spayed, so each month, she would jump over the fence to go have sex. Then she would come back pregnant.

The crazy thing about her was she attracted so many different dogs. During the nighttime, we'd hear dogs around our homes, trying to get to her. We wanted her to mate with a purebred German Shepherd. We would bring him to the crib, but it didn't matter to Leslie. She would not let him. He was a little on the old side; there was gray hair on his chin. Maybe that was the reason; maybe she had a thing about old dogs. But she would not mate with him at all.

She didn't mind letting all the stray dogs have a go. There was one time when I caught her with a stray in the alley behind our house. I was so mad; I grabbed a few rocks and tossed them near her. I didn't hit her or the other dog. I just wanted them to stop! Instead of pulling away from each other, Leslie began to run, and the other dog too, as they had been in the middle of… you get the picture. I ran after them for three blocks. Three blocks! I was so annoyed at that.

One time I remember being outside with Leslie when someone from the neighborhood showed up with their Pitbull.

Ola: The guy was a gang member.

Bola: I don't remember which gang, but he was a member. His dog was big, scary, and vicious looking. We had Leslie, a small German Shepherd mix. This dude said his dog could beat the crap out of my dog. I knew Leslie could hold her own. Looking back on it, I know you aren't supposed to do it, but back then, I just wanted to show that dude Leslie could take on his dog and put him in his place. Leslie really held her own. She may have been a small German Shepherd mix, but she was a tough dog. She showed that dog who was the boss. She really gave him the business!

Ola: She sure did! She showed that guy his badass Pitbull wasn't as tough as he thought he was. I don't know what happened to that dog or the guy. He never asked for a rematch. Leslie may have been small, but she didn't hesitate when we told her to attack that Pitbull. She was a tough dog.

Bola: Leslie was a good dog when she wasn't out chasing boys. She would not attack a human. We could get her to attack another dog if we felt threatened, but she wouldn't attack a human even if we had said for her to. I don't know what happened to her. I came home one day, and she was gone. I asked my mom, and she said she took her and let her off up the highway somewhere. I don't know if she really did that, but Leslie was gone.

Ola: After Leslie, we had two purebred German Shepherds, a boy and a girl. The boy was all black and brown. He was a good-looking dog. The girl had light colored hair beige or tan-colored. She was a very beautiful dog. They had babies, beautiful babies. Surprisingly, the girl, Robin, was calmer about the babies. The father, Robert, was the protective one. He would run around trying to bite anyone who came near them. He would have a fit if anyone got near the fence. He was a gentle animal as long as he didn't have his pups nearby. He was a overprotective father!

One time we took him for a walk in the park. There was this dude jogging by. He got too close to Robert, and Robert went into protective mode. He didn't bite him, thank God. He literally ripped the man's jogging suit off. We didn't take him or Robin to the park again. Thankfully, the man wasn't injured and didn't report it.

We ended up giving most of the babies away. While we were in Nigeria, my mom gave Robin away. She kept Robert. He was still with her when we came back from Nigeria. He had gotten so big while we were gone. Not just big, humongous. Robert was all bite and no bark. He wouldn't fight other dogs, but he was vicious towards humans. He truly was an amazing dog.

Bola: I have always been a prankster. A lot of my family are. I just love to play pranks on people, even as a kid. When we lived on the Southside, our parents went out to eat; not sure why without us, but they left us at home. We were watching a movie in our parents' room. I went to Ola's room and opened the window, then ran back to my parent's room where my siblings were. I said, "Oh my God, I just saw someone, someone inside our house! Someone was climbing through the window!"

Ola saw the window was open and got scared. I was like, "Oh my God!" We were freaking out. Then we called the police. They came and checked the surroundings. They didn't see anybody. My parents eventually came home. I never told them what happened. Not back then. I have recently told them, and I guess everyone else now.

Over the past few years, race has become a very hot topic. From wrongful deaths to police corruption, there is always something wrong. By no means do I think anything I say or do will change the issue alone, but my voice added to many others, can start a change. As a child growing up half in Chicago and half in Nigeria, I have seen the race issues in both countries. Race issues aren't just in the United States.

Growing up, when I was amongst my black friends because I was Nigerian, they would call me 'African Booty Snatcher' or just say you're

'African' in a way that made it sound like a slur. I was a little ashamed hearing those. I was proud, but it made me feel less then. I was Nigerian or I'm African, but I was made to feel like I was less than them.

The neighborhood in Southside we lived in was predominately Hispanic. That was the first time I felt like adults were looking down on me. They had a way of making me feel like I was less than them because of my heritage. I had felt a touch of racism in school through the years, but never had an adult made me feel that way.

These parents would look at their child and give some sort of signal, and the child would walk away or stop playing with me. I didn't know it at the time, but I did notice the way their children would move away from me. Being a minority as well, you would think they wouldn't be that way, but that just showed me race issues happen between all races, not just black and white.

We lived next door to a Hispanic family. They had a little Mexican dog they kept in their yard by a gate. The family had daughters, and as soon as we moved next door, they changed their metal fence to a tall wooden one so we couldn't see into their yard, and their daughters couldn't see into ours. My first thought was, 'Damn, are we that bad? Is there something wrong with us?' Thinking back on it, they weren't worried about us; it must have been their daughters they thought would come over to us that had them worried. How could they be worried about us; they didn't know us.

I was walking by this white family's gate, and the man said for me to go back to Africa. I remember at that time thinking, why did I have to go back to Africa? I wasn't born there. I was an American citizen. If he was implying that my family, my race, came from Africa, then wouldn't it reason that if I wasn't supposed to be in America because of my ancestors, he shouldn't be either? I could have told him to go back to Europe as his ancestors were from there, not the United States any more than mine were.

This is one of those things that people with issues about different races don't realize. When saying things like going back to Africa or Mexico or wherever they need to check their family tree. Unless you are of Native American blood, you are not from what is now the United States.

So, the next time you want to say to a black person they need to go back to Africa or a Hispanic person they need to go back to Spain or Mexico, or an Asian person to go back to Japan or China or wherever remember one thing, we are all immigrants to this great land, unless one of the Native American tribes that were here before any of us is in your family tree!

My parents raised me with good morals and to welcome all races and cultures. This kind of treatment went against what we had learned, but it was something that we would encounter all our lives.

Ola: Maybe it was because I was older, but these things didn't faze me that much. I knew I was not inferior to anyone. I was confident in who I was from an early age. I wasn't oblivious to the way I was treated by some people because of my heritage, but I didn't let it bother me. It did hurt me, but I didn't let it affect how I saw myself or my family. We grew up around whites, blacks, Hispanics, and a mixture of people. We adapted to whatever scene we faced. Regardless of the attitude of those that surrounded us, we did what we had to. That is how life is; no matter what race, you just have to do what you have to do.

Bola: It affected me differently. I think that is one of the reasons I would have outbursts in school or on field trips. Wanting to hang out or play with kids and then have their parents have them leave or just straight ignore me hurt. I never felt like I had to prove myself. I didn't try to fit in to make things better; I concentrated on getting good grades and being the best I could be. It is kind of the same way today in my life. I always try to be the best I can be.

Ola: Our father always told us when we were younger, whatever we do, we should be the best in it. We should strive to be the best in it. To never chase girls, to chase money.

Bola: I always told my mother when there was something I wanted, I would say, "Mom, don't worry when I'm older, I'm gonna be rich, and I'm gonna buy you and I whatever you want." She will always say, "By God's grace, by God's grace."

Ola: Our last name, Osundairo, has an important meaning. "Osun" means water. "Dairo" means stop or keep in place. In our history, if a firstborn child was dying, they went into the water. A deity kept them from dying them to stop dying. Osundairo means to stop the children.

My brother already told you my father and my mother's side are royalty. My father has six siblings: four boys and two girls. My grandfather, on my mother's side, had many wives. I don't know how many wives exactly. He had countless children. We have a very large family as a result!

Bola: Even with all we saw involving race, I never wished I was anyone else; I wished I was similar to them, but I never wished I was anyone else or any other race. I am who I am meant to be. The Almighty made me. Therefore, I am how I should be. I may have wished I was similar sometimes to others, but not once did I ever wish that I was not who I am.

Ola: I agree with what my brother said. I know that I am who I was meant to be. The person that I was born to be. The Almighty made me as he made my brother. As he made you and everyone else. And we are who we are meant to be because that is how it is. He made me the man I am.

Bola: I remember this lesson my parents were trying to teach us. It really stood out amongst other lessons. We were living in Southside, and my parents called both of us into their rooms. They gave my brother a headband, which was the cool thing to have at this time. The NBA players used to wear them, so kids really liked them. My parents gave Ola one, and then they told us to leave their room. I got upset because they didn't give me one. I stormed out with an attitude. Why could he have one, and I couldn't? That wasn't fair! Why call both of us to them if only one was to be gifted with a headband?

They called me back to their room and reprimanded me for that. They wanted to know why I had an attitude. I wouldn't say why. Eventually, they gave me my own headband. It was white with a black *Nike* sign on it.

I was happy, obviously, but it taught me that I should always delay my upset feelings just in case I am being tested, haha. Most importantly, it taught me that I should be patient, ask questions and not jump to conclusions. They had many ways they would teach us lessons. Of course, for the most part, we didn't know it was a lesson until afterward. To this day, I remember that when I am quick to anger or get upset about something. I pause in my anger to think before I react. I take a deep breath and then reply. Replying in the heat of anger can make things worse. Think before you speak.

Chapter Four

HIGH SCHOOL

Bola: In 2005, we went to Nigeria. My parents told me we were going to Nigeria, that's it. I wasn't told if it was for a visit or to stay. We packed a lot of clothes to go there. It seemed like we were going to be there for a little while, at least. I remember thinking to myself; there was this girl I liked that lived next to us. We were just getting around to talking, and now we're leaving!

We stepped off the plane, and it was like someone slapped me across the face with a burning limb! The heat was scorching! I wanted nothing more than to turn around and instruct the pilot to fly me home! I didn't have time to stew over my being in a country that had to be as hot as the fires of hell!

My grandparents lived in a big white house they called God's Grace. My grandmother and grandfather named it God's Grace because they believe with God's Grace, we can become the person the Almighty wants us to be. My grandfather had God's Grace placed upon the house in the hope that we remember God loves us and shows us His grace in many ways. This home is so much more than four walls. It is a welcoming embrace from our grandparents and the Almighty.

Within those walls, love, faith, joy, and sorrow abide. In life, you can't have the first three without the last. Faith, like love and joy, surrounds us daily. It's there on a sunny day or upon a newborn baby's smile. With every sunny day or newborn's smile, there is sorrow somewhere in this world. With each moment of sorrow, a moment of loss, there is comfort from the Almighty. In these moments of loss, there are those who offer you love, faith, and joy in the memories of the one you have lost.

The Almighty fills God's Grace and those who encounter it with a loving, forgiving heart. A heart filled with the Almighty, and His grace fills them. My grandparents instilled these beliefs in my brother and me. We strive to live this way daily.

We stayed on the third floor of God's Grace. I remember having to walk up a long staircase just to get to our flat. Maybe my grandparents thought we needed to be a little closer to the Almighty than others in the house.

There were two parlors and a living room sort of room. One parlor was only for my grandparents. We weren't allowed in there. The other parlor was ours and anyone else who lived in God's Grace. There were times when we would be served refreshments. The first time we got to Nigeria they brought us 'La Casera', an apple-flavored soft drink. I can't recall what it was at the moment, but when I opened it, there were ants on it! I said I was good, thanks anyway. No way was I eating ants!

Upon reaching God's Grace we were bombarded with people! There were so many people anxious to see us! Aunts, Uncles, cousins, you name it, they were there! This was my first look at how big my family was, and they were all there to see us! It was a welcome home reception sort of thing. One by one, we met them. I know I was told names and how we were related, but at the time, I couldn't remember more than a handful of them. They were all happy to meet us. Family is really big in Nigeria.

My brothers and I were the older cousins, which was great! It was a great experience to have someone looking up to us. It might be okay to live there for a while, after all. We had game consoles we could share with our cousins. It would be nice to have others close to my age that weren't my siblings!

Everyone gave us a warm welcome, but they made it known that we were different than regular Nigerians. Our parents and grandparents were born in Nigeria, but my siblings and I weren't. We were Nigerian but not considered the same Nigerian as the family born there!

We were always different! No matter where we went, we never fit in! Most of the time, a remark or a dig at us about being American-born was done in a playful way. I knew they were just teasing but insulting someone in a playful manner is still an insult when you get down to it!

We were too American! We were in Nigeria now! Our accents were funny! These were similar to the taunts we'd hear in America! I quickly learned to speak without an accent!

My parents had some sort of arrangement where at least one of them was with us in whatever country we were in. On this trip, my mother remained in America, and my father came with us. I am closest to my mother. Mothers go to bat for their children more than a father does. I remember that being a big disadvantage to me, not having my mother there. I was closer to my mother than my father.

My dad kind of allowed the aunts, the women of the house, to take care of the children. I guess that was the traditional way. Taking care of the children was the role of the woman. Had my mother been there, that would have been what she did.

From the moment it was decided we would go to Nigeria for Ola's high school years and my middle school days, my grandfather had been searching for the perfect boarding school for us. He took us to a few after we arrived. One of them allowed no nonsense! The school was huge and way too strict!

We took an entrance exam just to see where we placed. If we failed, they still would have accepted us there. They knew my grandfather, that is why they accepted us into that school. Thankfully we did not go there! If we had, we would have just been a number.

The school we ended up going to was called Latinos Comprehensive College in Ikotun. They were just starting their boarding program. We were in the lucky set of students they started with. Maybe lucky is the wrong word. Being the guinea pig for this could be good or bad!

Since it was a new program, there weren't girl dorms and boy dorms. There weren't that many of us at the time. We all shared one dorm or hostel, as it's called there. We were sharing with the girls! The teenage boy in me was loving this!

At the school, we were treated very well. I think it was because we were foreigners, which was unusual. I have found most people, strangers, treat foreigners well for the most part. There are those who don't like foreigners that don't hesitate to show that. I think those that treat you kindly do so thinking you have money or maybe, like me, they were raised to treat others with respect regardless of who they are and where they came from.

I learned a lot about myself and who I wanted to be there. This was my formative years. I truly believe I am who I am because of what I learned at that school and God's Grace.

In Nigeria, we started school quickly. At first, I was upset that we were going to boarding school. I thought first you bring us to Nigeria and make us stay; then you ship us off to school with no parents, no guardian. What's going on?

I hadn't heard of boarding schools until this. Here I was in a country I barely knew, and now I was stuck with a bunch of boys and girls that I knew nothing about. Had my brother not been there with me, I don't know how things would have turned out.

Looking back, the time I spent there helped me learn how to face life. Starting with buying provisions like powdered milk, cereal, and things like that. I could eat them as snacks and whatnot. They would give me pure water in a sachet. You don't drink the tap water over there! At least I didn't. To drink over there, you either had a sachet of water or you drank bottled water. Other people drank the water, but I bought pure water in two sachets.

My parents sent me off with 2500 naira at the time. That, in today's dollars, would be $5.43! Not a lot of money at all! Things are cheaper in Nigeria, but even so, that money was gone fast! I had to learn how to make it last. Even though I did, I still ran out! That's the first time I learned sometimes you have to make the money you have to stretch or find another way to get food!

When the money was gone, I had to tell my mother or father. Whoever I spoke to at that point was in the country with us. Sometimes there would be more money. Sometimes there wouldn't.

Eventually, the boys were moved across the street to our own building. That was when we got a housemaster. He was the person charged with keeping us in line in our building. Usually, it was a teacher that I liked or didn't. It didn't matter either way. My first housemaster was my computer teacher. I liked him as a computer teacher. As a housemaster, he was okay. The other boys and I gave him hell, but he gave as good as he got! If the housemasters were fun like that, the days were great. If not, it could be hell!

Even though I liked my housemaster, I still had a disdain for authority. If someone tried to tell me what to do, I had to do something I wasn't supposed to do. I didn't really like living at the hostel. I had no choice to live anywhere else.

I had to create a schedule so I didn't miss anything. I woke up at 7:00 AM. I then make my way two miles to school. I ate what little there was to eat. After getting a boys-only hostel, the food somehow was less than before. The cook would cook eleven eggs for twenty-two boys! That's crazy to me!

In Nigeria, schools aren't the same as in America. There we have Junior Secondary School and Senior Secondary School. There are JS1-JS3 and SS1-SS3. Ola was in SS1. I was the youngest in JS1. The thing about being in JS1 is you get the last call or last pickings on everything, including the food. That meant all the seniors and then JS2-JS3 had their food. What was left was then divided amongst the JS1. As you can imagine, there wasn't much to eat.

In school, I wasn't allowed to call my brother by his name. I had to refer to him as Senior Binjo. As seniors, Ola could command me and my fellow classmates. If we didn't obey, there were consequences. The seniors liked having us clean their rooms and do their laundry for them!

Knowing my opinion on authority, Ola knew this would be an issue for me.

In Nigeria, they are very big on respect, not just with your elders but with everyone. For instance, when I greet my grandparents, I had to lie down to greet them. It's called prostrate. We bend down and bow our heads to greet them. It depends on who they are as to how far you kneel or bow your head.

We were disciplined if we didn't prostrate. I remember my grandfather gave me a little tap one time because I didn't greet him. I didn't intentionally forget; it was just because we weren't used to it at the time.

When meeting my aunts and uncles, I wasn't required to lie down, but I had to kneel and bow my head. The same was done for me when I was the oldest. The new generation bows when greeting me.

There was this one time I couldn't take any more. I got mad at the housemaster when he told me to do something. I said no. When he wanted to punish us, if you could call the beating, he'd give us punishment; he would lock the gate keeping us in. I climbed the gate while he was trying to come outside. I started throwing rocks at the gate. There were little holes in it, so I was throwing rocks to prevent him from coming out. I knew he was scared; he was running back and forth. I felt exhilarated. The housemaster reported me to the proprietor.

There was a male proprietor, and his wife was the principal of the school. After the gate incident, I expected punishment would be waiting for me. But I didn't get into trouble. The proprietor and his wife liked me. Other people would get into trouble, but I didn't.

We switched housemasters though I don't remember why. Maybe because of the gate incident. The new one was also the French teacher. I thought the headmaster before him was an issue; this guy was worse! He had a wicked streak. I remember wanting to eat, but he said I couldn't. He withheld the food, saying I couldn't eat until I did something. I don't remember why. Sometimes he did so without a reason.

There were thirteen of us at this point. When you put thirteen boys together and withhold their food, you better be ready for the consequences! We began to orchestrate a plan on how to get the food. The thirteen of us thought dressing in hoodies and giving off a menacing creepy vibe would scare him into giving us our food. We walked in there like we were gangsters about to whack everyone in the place as mobsters did. We wanted our food! It wasn't funny at the time, but looking back on it, I can't help but laugh. There was no way that man would have been scared of teenagers. But at the time, I knew everything! When I really knew nothing.

There was a glass panel nearby. He grabbed it and slammed it on the table. It shattered, and glass went everywhere, as did we. Instead of us scaring him, he scared us! We did what a teenager does. We ran to the next available adult! In this instance, it was the proprietor. Each of us told him what had happened and how we didn't like that man, that he scared us. We didn't feel safe with that man!

That night, they had us sleep in their hallway. No way were we sleeping in the same place as that man! The proprietor's house had a huge compound. There was a little land separating the proprietor's house and the hostel. I don't remember how many nights we slept there, but eventually, they got rid of that housemaster. Good riddance!

I was washing my clothes in the backyard; I guess I wasn't supposed to be washing at the time. Maybe I was supposed to be studying, I don't remember, but he came over to me and slapped me. It pissed me off! I wanted to slap him back, to hurt him as he had me. But I knew I couldn't fight him. I was by myself. That had nothing to do with why I didn't knock him on his ass! I knew if I attempted to return his unwanted gift, I'd be in a heap of trouble! Hitting a housemaster would no doubt have landed me in serious trouble! While his treatment of me would have gone unpunished. It wouldn't matter if I was favored by the proprietor and his wife.

Boarding school taught us about more than books. That is where I learned to play soccer and ping pong. We played soccer in the backyard with no shoes most of the time. We had a lot of foot injuries as a result, but that didn't stop us from playing that way. We used to play ping pong in the front of our compound. It was almost as fun as soccer and had a whole lot fewer injuries!

Soccer is my favorite sport now. Even though I love boxing, soccer is my favorite sport.

My last housemaster, Mr. Ogunbiyi was cool. He was the most laid-back and relaxed housemaster we ever had. But at times, he could be too strict! He liked to lock our soccer ball up. He knew playing soccer relieved our stress and gave us something to do. That didn't stop him, though! We may be young, but schoolwork can be stressful! A game or two of soccer not only gave us a chance to get some exercise. It became a sort of game to figure out how we could get the ball back.

In my second year, JS2, there was a new JS1 student from France. His name was Jide. He was a lighter complexion than me. I believe his mom is white, but his dad is Nigerian. He was a cool dude. He was good with his hands. I saw him create a snail farm once. It was cool!

When our housemaster locked up our ball, Jide created a hole in the ceiling of the closet. That enabled us to go to the housemaster's closet ceiling. Then one of us would go through and get the ball. When the headmaster wasn't there. The man never found out as he didn't go into his closet. Eventually, we were able to make a second set of keys. After that, we no longer used the hole in the ceiling. As far as I know, those holes are still there.

One night around 1:00 am, we began making as much noise as possible with glass, aluminum plates, and anything else we could find. We started throwing it at his door. He got scared and locked his door. We started making more noise and banging on his door over and over. He was scared. I don't know what we would have done if we got into his room. I think Jide was going to beat him up. I honestly think so. The man being scared made us feel good. After all, he'd done, it was nice to have a good feeling. By this time, there were twenty-two of us. He was outnumbered, and he knew it. He couldn't punish us as he didn't know exactly who it was.

Jide was adventurous but we were good. He had no reason to have issues with us. The first time I witnessed black magic was when Jide cooked it up. I don't know who he bought it from, a spiritual doctor, I guess. He cooked it up on a little plate they gave him. It was seeds or something like that. He had to say something that whoever it was used on would make them agree to do what he wanted.

He used it on one of our housemasters, the replacement for the one we were scared of. That dude wouldn't let us go out once he locked the gate to our hostel. We wanted to get some food down the street after he locked the gate. He took pleasure in telling us no when we asked. Jide used his black magic on him. Jide told him he wanted him to open the gate. I wouldn't have believed it if I hadn't seen it with my own eyes! That man opened the gate!

When I was eleven or twelve years old, we were playing table tennis in the front yard. Suddenly I hear someone screaming 'I am not a thief! I am not a thief!' I was like, what the hell is this? About thirty to forty seconds later, I heard loud noises. I looked back, and it was a gang of people, at least thirty, running after this dude! It was crazy! This gang of people looked like those you see in movies carrying pitchforks and lanterns! These people were chasing that dude!

I finally went out the gate. Down the block, I saw he had been tied to a motorcycle, and a gang of people were stoning him. Then they tied only his ankles to the motorcycle and dragged him down to a swamp that was nearby. Then they put tires on him and burned him alive. That was the first time I saw jungle justice.

With jungle justice, you can feel bad for the person, but nobody dares try to intervene. If you did, you would find yourself right beside them. Witnessing that was hard. I might not agree with what I saw, but I also knew that it could happen to me if I chose to steal. He had been limping because he jumped out of a two or three-story building. He had been with three or four other people. They escaped.

Chapter Five

HOSTEL LIVING

Bola: The first time I was in a hostel, I came in close contact with the Islam religion. Our proprietor and principal were Muslim, as were many of the students. At times they would take us with them to worship and pray on Sundays. I was pretty close with the proprietor and the principal's children. They would come over and play with us. There were times when the oldest son Uncle Yinka, would try to discipline us. Once, we did something to the housemaster, and Uncle Yinka whooped us. Even so, I still liked him. The youngest boy was Uncle Tunde. There was another son, Uncle Agboola, and two daughters. Uncle Agboola was my favorite. One of the girls, Auntie Odun, had polio. She was the oldest. She would look out for us. Their youngest Auntie Bukky, I had a crush on. She was older than me, good-looking, and filled out in all the right places. I didn't stand a chance. They weren't our aunts or uncles. In Nigeria, it is a show of respect to prefix the name of someone who is older than you. I am called Uncle Bola by anyone younger than me.

They would fast for Ramadan. I didn't know what Ramadan was until learning of it from them. Ramadan is a period of introspection and communal prayer. During this time, they would fast all day for twenty-nine to thirty days. You are only allowed to eat before the first rays of dawn and after the last of the setting sun each day. I fasted with them. I would eat before the sun came up and wait until it went down to eat again.

I prayed five times a day. They did that as one of the five pillars of Islam. I wasn't a Muslim, but I found this to be a great experience. I would break my fast at the principal's house. They had plenty of food. One reason I would do this was because there was so much food. I was able to eat until I was full. Since we weren't able to eat much due to the number of boys and the small amount of food, this was a great relief to me.

I was always hungry, except for Ramadan. It was the only time I actually ate as much as I wanted! Our food at the school was cooked by the cook, but for Ramadan, my Auntie Odun would do the cooking. She cooked with love. The chef at the school would cook for our hostel, and then we'd take it to the hostel two miles away. At times I would eat some of the meat they gave us. There were twenty-two kids and twenty-two pieces of meat. When we would get the food to the hostel, they would see there wasn't enough meat, and they'd say we had to go to the principal's house down the street to get meat. We would get meat and eggs from there. Eggs and meat were a luxury. Occasionally there would be spaghetti, rice, and swallow–Cassava is a root soaked in water for three to four days.

School in Nigeria was a culture shock. My teachers were allowed to flog us. They had the right to whoop you at school! I knew that, but as I have mentioned, I'm a rebel. I don't deal with authority very well, but I couldn't do anything with my teachers. I had to take the flogging. There was no one there to save me. It was up to me to save myself.

I had to be on my best behavior when it came to those teachers. They enjoyed flogging the students too much. Certain teachers would whoop your ass with a bamboo stick. There were one or two who would tie together two bamboo sticks and flog you. The math/chemistry teacher would flog you on your calves. One teacher flogged your hand! Imagine what that feels like!

After getting one flogging, you tried not to get another! If you were tardy, disruptive in class, or missing your assignments, you would be punished. Classes in Nigeria are different. You get graded by two mini-tests called CA-Continuous Assessments, and then by a final exam at the end of the semester and tests. You had to really study to pass these tests. There was no time for joking or playing around.

In Nigeria, I was a social being. I was well-liked by girls, guys, and teachers. The boys wanted to be me! The girls wanted to date me! And the teachers liked me because I was fun, if somewhat a rebel. I remember many of my teachers from back then. There was this one teacher, Mr. Egunjobi. He taught science, so naturally, he was my favorite teacher. He was also bribable with buns and soda pop. All a student had to do was give him one of each, and he would adjust your grade a little. I had good grades, so I never had to worry, but a few of those I know kept a bun and a soda pop on hand, just in case.

I remember once when it was time for school fees to be paid, and everyone was to stand outside. The principal would come by, and if the dues weren't paid, she'd say, 'You didn't pay! You have to go home!'

Once, our parents hadn't paid on time, and we should have been sent home, but the proprietor and the principal favored us and would let us go back inside, knowing payment would come through. They had a little favoritism where we were concerned.

After what seemed like forever of having to walk to the hostel from the school and vice versa, we finally got a bus! The bus not only took us back and forth to school, but we were also able to go on field trips! The field trips in America were fun. I couldn't wait to see where we would go!

One of the field trips was to a seaport. I don't remember which seaport or what we did while there, but that made a mark on me. From that moment on, I vowed I would one day own a seaport. This is one of my goals that I will make a reality! I don't know where I will own it, but it will be somewhere in Africa or West Africa. I don't want to own a shipping company; I want to own the actual seaport. There is something about seeing that place and how the commerce of the area needs a seaport. If there wasn't one, the goods that were imported and exported there wouldn't happen.

Every morning we had an assembly where we would sing our national anthem. Then we'd hear the daily announcements and have the morning prayer. First is the Christian prayer, followed by a Muslim prayer. Sometimes we did the opposite and had the Muslim prayer first. During the Muslim prayer, some of the students would make fun of some of the words because they sounded similar to the names of other things. I always found the prayer to be pretty. After assembly, we were to go to different classes, much like high school in America. The difference is we remain in our class, and the teachers switch.

The music teacher and I had an issue. He was that one teacher I couldn't win over. I was playing soccer, and somehow, the ball hit his door. It wasn't intentional. He slapped me and then told me to kneel down so he could punish me. I may be a rebel, but I knew I had to kneel down. Every part of me wanted to refuse! It would be different if I had done something to deserve what was to come, but it was truly an accident! Not that he cared to listen. He went to his office to get something, and I ran. School was out, and students were leaving. I mingled in with them, hoping he wouldn't see me!

I saw him come outside with his cane. He saw me and came after me. I ran, scared for my life. He was fast! He was catching up to me. I did the only thing I could think to do. I jumped in the gutter. Thank God the gutter wasn't wet! He kept looking. A few of the seniors and my brother showed up. I think that was the reason he didn't jump in the gutter with me. If he had, I would have had to fight. And he would have whooped me with that cane.

Ola: I was the reason that the teacher didn't give Bola that whooping. I stopped that. As Bola said, we were punished with bamboo, but there was this other wooden stick thing they used too. It was round and of different sizes. It was kind of like three extension cords put together, but it was wooden. It would give very little when it hit you. And it hurt like hell!

Bola: Eventually, I got in a little trouble, but not what it could have been, as the principal saved me. From that moment on, I had a beef with that teacher.

There were some parts of the Muslim faith I found interesting. I believe in Christ, our Lord and Savior. The Muslims believe Jesus was a prophet of the Almighty. They are very disciplined. As Christians, we pray and do our best to live the right way. Muslims pray five times a day. If you don't, you can't consider yourself a Muslim. If you don't fast during Ramadan, you can't consider yourself a Muslim. It's a religion orthopraxy—belief in the belief that the right action is as important as religious faith. I found the Muslim faith interesting. I have chosen to observe some of their ways.

I liked being in Nigeria, but I resented it as well. I don't think it was the American in me. It was more who I am. Where we lived in the Southside, we came in contact with gangs on a daily basis. I think that the fear of what might happen if we remained there was a part of the reason my parents took us to Nigeria when they did.

In Nigeria, there aren't gangs like in America. In Nigeria, there are confraternities. In the States, you have fraternities where you find friendships that form a bond, almost like brothers. Fraternities in Nigeria are secretive students and groups. The members, at some point in their lives, have done some form of violence and organized crime.

My identity, my family, and my history are very important to me. Our heritage that we come from royalty is known in Nigeria. Because of this, we were treated differently when in Nigeria. My mother's maiden name is Adeoye. When Ade is in your last name, that means crown or signifies you are from royal blood. On my father's side, my great-grandfather was the first judge, and our people were part of those that brought the first church to our town.

The hardest part of living in Nigeria was what happened to my skin. I would get these wounds all over my body. I'm talking about gross pus-filled places on my skin! It didn't affect my siblings the same. A few of them had something similar but not as bad. There was something there that affected me. I never could figure out what. Thankfully that stopped the more time I spent in Nigeria. I think I still have a few black scars from that.

Even at school, I tried not to shit because the bathroom was filthy. Just going in there, the flies touched me! I was disgusted! I do not like dirty toilets! To this day, I will not shit on a dirty toilet. I won't even put something on the toilet and go. No way! I stand over it! I even peed outside! There were these banana trees out back that I would use.

Sometimes the soccer ball would go back there. The ball would get all nasty; then the seniors would ask who would poop out there. I never told them it was me. I was being discreet about it, but I wasn't comfortable with the toilets. I didn't shower in the bathroom, I showered outside. I didn't pee in them, either. They were so nasty. It makes me cringe just talking about it!

I had to be sneaky when finding somewhere amongst the banana trees! I didn't want to get caught! If I saw anyone or heard anyone, I wouldn't go, but eventually, I had to! I have never told anyone that! I guess I just did!

The mosquitoes were crazy in Nigeria! For some reason, I attracted them like bees to honey! My blood or scent must attract them. It must be my winning personality! Everyone loves me, including the mosquitos!

Finally, my time to return to the States arrived! I would begin American high school when I got back. It was decided Ola would remain and finish high school. It was basically what we would call his senior year. My father flew to the States with my sisters, and I.

I was ready to get home! I was happy about seeing my friends on the south side and catching up. I was counting down the days.

It wasn't until I got home I found myself on the Northside. Everything was new. I had no friends from that area. I was a little disappointed. I wanted to go to school at Gurdon S. Hubbard High School with all the people I'd known before Nigeria. I asked if I could take the train and go there. No! Not an option! I would be going to Lake View High.

When I went to Nigeria, I skipped a grade. Upon returning to the US, I was in ninth grade while all my friends were just starting eighth grade. Had I gotten to attend high school on the south side, I wouldn't have had any classes with my friends after all. At least I would have been able to see them at lunch. My mother wanted me to start school immediately. I didn't have a chance to catch up with anyone before I was enrolled in Lake View High! She had to go to the Board of Education and give them my transcripts from Nigeria, and I was good to go.

After my time in Nigeria, I had an accent. People made fun of it. I had to put up with name-calling and noises. I guess it would be considered bullying, but I didn't see it that way. I tried not to let them get to me.

The noises were the most annoying. Honestly, the teasing I had upon moving to Nigeria was more inventive than this. It wasn't like I could say,

'Get better insults! Nigeria puts you to shame!' That would have caused all kinds of issues. Teenagers live to cause trouble and are very competitive! I tried not to let it bother me. In ways, this was a pattern in my life. I grew up in a neighborhood of Hispanics, whites, and blacks, but I was never fully accepted because my heritage was Nigerian until they got to know me. In Nigeria, I was different because I came from America and had an accent. I came back to America, and once more, I didn't fit in because now I had a Nigerian accent. It couldn't make anyone happy. Good thing that wasn't something I had to do!

It seemed like I had to constantly adapt to and fit in. As a result, I always had a chip on my shoulder. I held myself to what my parents had always told me. I am a Prince. I had a strong background and a strong culture. I was a descendant of royalty. I was the great-great-grandson of the first judge of our whole region. I was a descendant of a big family. To live by doing what was needed to be the best we could be.

Many times, I was questioned by my friends or acquaintances on how I could be a prince, and Ola could be too. What were we Princes of? I didn't know the answer at first, but I learned. I am not afraid to ask questions to learn what I don't know. In America, the kids would ask if my being a prince was like being the president's kid or if I was a prince the way that the Queen's grandsons in England are. It wasn't something many could understand.

I was a prince within my culture. A prince of my people. Ola is a descendant of the same family; therefore, he is a prince. For those who don't have similar cultures, it can be hard to understand.

I am a pretty easygoing guy. As a result, people gravitate to me. They may not understand my heritage and how I could be a prince, but they wanted to be friends anyway. The girls were easier to impress than the guys. The girls liked that I was different. They thought it was cool I had an accent. While the guys were making fun of my accent, the girls were swooning over it.

The most popular noise the guys could make while attempting to make fun of me was making a blowing sound like blowing a dart. No doubt they had seen different tribes in movies, like that one about the archeologist that is constantly getting himself in some trouble. If you watch those movies, you see the native tribes and hear them blowing in a piece of bamboo to shoot darts. This was the sound the students of Lake View High used as an insult to me. Personally, I found it showed their ignorance more than insulting me.

They have this image of chasing cheetahs and shit like that. I've been asked if I lived with animals. A hostel? What was that? I would explain it was sort of like a dorm room. Someone in the group would speak up and say something like, 'Isn't that the name of a movie? I'm pretty sure there is a movie called *Hostel*.' I would roll my eyes and try to explain in terms they could understand.

After the newness of my being from a country they most likely couldn't find on a map, my life turned normal. Well, normal as it could be, I guess.

Chapter Six

I KNOW YOU MISSED ME!

Ola: When I first arrived in Nigeria, I thought it was going to be for a visit, then back to America. I had plans. I was going to be a professional football player. I had to be in America for that. I knew I would have to play ball through high school and college. I needed to do this to go after my career as a bodybuilder. To find out I would be spending my high school years in Nigeria made me very unhappy.

I remember walking off the plane and being hit with the heat like I'd never felt before. I wasn't looking forward to what was to come. First, football was gone, and now it was hot, the kind of hot you can cook eggs on the street. Hot didn't begin to describe that heat! I had dealt with hot in the States. This was more like an inferno kind of heat!

Upon arriving at Osundairo Street at the family's home, God's Grace, I found my father, and my siblings and I would be on the third floor of the three-story building. My father's youngest brother would be there as well. The building my grandfather owned, on the street that was named after him, Osundairo.

My father, his children, and his youngest brother occupied the top floor of the three-story building. Two other siblings occupied units on the ground floor. The rest were rented out as office spaces. My grandparents had a gate man and two maids that cooked and cleaned for them and us.

Every morning my grandfather would ring a bell, and we would know to meet in the living room, where he would lead us in prayer. He would do the same each night. Our living space, our home, is the same as an apartment building in the States. For some reason, people seem to think our living arrangements are in huts or something.

There had been so many kids born since I'd been there. It was great to meet them, but knowing I wasn't going back to America made me sad. Eventually, I got used to everything and embraced being there. There is something about being with family and knowing your history, your origins. You have this feeling of belonging and comfort.

Video games were my thing in America. I was born in the video gaming era. To this day, when I can find time, I play. I wasn't close with my cousins since I didn't see them that much, even when living in Nigeria. I was closest with my brother, with Bola. We had the latest consoles and video games in America. When we moved to Nigeria, we took our Xbox with us. The plug on an American Xbox isn't compatible with Nigerian power outlets. We had a converter, but when we weren't there, we took it with us. We didn't want our cousins to play with it without us being there. They plugged it straight into the wall and fried our Xbox.

Bola: It was a very upsetting time for us. We had prayer sessions for that box!

Ola: We had a gate man and two maids that cooked and cleaned for my grandparents and whatever the kids needed as well. In the mornings, we would gather in the living room when my grandfather rang the bell. He would lead prayer every night and every morning.

It was summer when I arrived in Nigeria. It gave me time to be with family before starting school. Then I was sent off to boarding school, three or four hours away from where my grandparents lived.

For growing young men, we were always hungry. There was never enough food which was very disheartening. But like Bola, when Ramadan came around, I noticed that after the Muslims were finished fasting every day, they would have a huge feast at the proprietors. So, we began to fast with the Muslims too. We were allowed to join in on the festivities. We even prayed with them and went to the mosque.

The food wasn't the reason we prayed and followed some of the Muslim traditions. It was a bonus to share in their breaking of the fast each day. I enjoy learning about things, including religion. I found a number of their customs interesting and chose to adopt them as my own, the way Bola did.

I got along with almost all of my teachers. Like my brother, I was well-liked. It has something to do with our demeanor, I think. In the way we treat people.

There was one teacher in particular, Mr. Osage, who all the students liked. In school, every morning, we sang the national anthem, followed by the Muslim and Christian prayers. I started there in SS1 and chose to study science instead of commerce or arts because my father was always pushing me to become a doctor.

The science students at school had to study physics, chemistry, biology, and advanced mathematics plans. I included English, computer, and geography. Between my studies, I stayed relatively active. I got into football which is known as soccer in America.

The restrooms at my school in Nigeria had the worst bathrooms! They were not up to my standards! I'm not being a diva; the bathrooms there are disgusting! The ones at the hostel are one of the worst I've ever seen. I wouldn't even shower in them; that's how bad they were!

I was the unlucky one who caught Malaria and got very sick. Sick to the point where I thought that I was going to die! I don't know if my family was notified or not, but if so, no one came to check on me. I didn't go to the hospital. I was on Malaria drugs and finally got through it. It was from those damn mosquitos! I swear they waited on me to walk outside, and then they just attacked!

My dad wanted me to be a doctor, as I mentioned earlier, so I took all the right courses, science studies, physics, advanced math, and computers. All the courses for a future as a doctor. At first, it was difficult. Education in Nigeria is very fast-paced. What the teacher does is read out of the textbook, and the students have to write out the whole textbook. It was the only way a student had one. If you failed to make notes of all the text, that was your problem. It was difficult at first to keep up, but I was able to acclimate pretty well and started doing better. Much to my father's dismay, I had no desire to be a doctor; that was all his vision. Being a doctor was never in my heart.

School in Nigeria is ten times or a hundred more difficult than in America. There is no time for slacking off in Nigeria. There are no links to help you get help online. Either you take excellent notes while the teacher is reading, or you are out of luck. Not to say anything negative about the teachings in America, but the students here aren't taught in such strict ways.

My grades weren't bad, but they weren't great in elementary school in America. I wasn't the best student, no matter the location, but I worked on it and got my grades up.

There was this one time Bola, and I made weights out of the only thing we had, concrete. When I don't have what I need, if there is a way to make it, I will usually do so. We needed weights to work out with. We had concrete. We used what we had to get what we needed. They weren't the best weights, but they did what we needed them to. Sometimes you have to improvise.

Bola mentioned Jide and black magic. This was something I had seen before but never participated in. A lot of the black magic calls for an animal of some sort. To make sure no one messes with their livestock, they have been known to place voodoo curses on them. People put curses and protective spells on their livestock and then let them roam around freely. If someone is brave enough to try and grab the animal, something will happen to them that day. At least, that's what I heard.

One night we caught one of the hostel mates stealing. That night we woke him up and dragged him out of bed. All of us were covered to hide our identity. We took him to the backyard, took all of his clothes off, and then took turns whooping him with a belt. Then we poured water on top of him and pretty much punished him.

The next-door neighbor, that always stares out the windows came out yelling we were a cult! Cult! Once we heard her come out, we all started running. We scattered and ran inside. She never reported us because we never heard anything from the proprietor or the principal. I guess she never snitched on us.

I had my first love when I was sixteen; I started dating Tosin. This girl broke my heart towards the end of the semester. We had only been dating a short time. I found out she was writing love letters back and forth with one of my hostel mates! The really crazy part is how I found out. Jide was going to the voodoo doctor, but before he did, he found this guy's book, my housemates. In this book were love letters between him and *my* girlfriend!

She was a good girl! Very innocent and shy! I had no idea how she was able to do what she did. She didn't kiss him or anything like that, but at that young age, telling somebody else that you love them was just wrong!

This book had Ju Ju incantations and black magic in it. There were a lot of notes full of black magic incantations. I think that was why she was writing him letters. I think he'd used that black magic on her. I just can't imagine a girl as innocent and shy as she would have written half of that.

My siblings left, and I stayed to finish my last year. My father stayed with me. I didn't mind being left behind. At the time, I had a girlfriend, and I didn't want to leave her. It was my parent's decision to leave me to finish school at sixteen and graduate. I would start college at seventeen in America.

My father remained with me. He started in politics at this time. He ran for mayor while we were there. Unfortunately, he didn't win.

In many ways, the last year flew by, but in other ways, it was the slowest of my life. As the time approached for me to leave, my grandmother and my aunt took me to my grandmother's and prayed over me. They gave me something special that I still have. Something that I will always treasure.

My experiences in Nigeria helped make me the man I am today. I also believe I found God, truly found him while in Nigeria. I read the Bible two times while there. We had prayers morning and night, and one night I was moved so much by the spirit I fell forward and hit my head on somebody's knee. Nobody checked up on me. I woke up a couple of seconds later and just went back to praying.

Looking back, I can tell that my parents' movements all through our lives were a step forward to improve their lives and ours. We started out in subsidized housing. My parents made decisions that took us from there to something more. My parents found new opportunities that would improve their lives and ours.

My most memorable moment in Nigeria was when I was fourteen. I lost my virginity to my housemaster's sister. I don't know if I would call it rape or not. She was twenty-four. She came to visit her family; this was our French housemaster. His sister had come to visit. She stayed at the hostel in his room with us.

She was there for two weeks or something like that. And there was a time when she had to leave early from school and come back to the house. She got me drunk, and we did what we did on the living room couch. The second time it happened, I think it was a weekend. I think the housemaster wasn't there and we did it in his room.

Looking back on it, I don't know if it can be considered rape, but she did get me drunk before the first time. I was a young boy, and she was a young woman; it could be considered taking advantage of me, I suppose. I don't remember feeling that way. To a fourteen-year-old, she was sophisticated. A cougar, I guess.

Chapter Seven

I'M BACK AMERICA

Ola: After three years, it was time to return home. Coming back to the United States was a bit of a culture shock all over again. It wasn't the easiest to get acclimated to home again. This was home, the place of my birth, but after three years in Nigeria, that was home as well. I had an accent again, only this time, it wasn't an American accent. I couldn't hear it, but anytime I spoke to somebody, they were quick to point it out.

It had been three years since I had seen him, but Robert, our German Shepard, had grown! A lot! But he didn't remember me. At all! For a couple of weeks, he had to wear a muzzle anytime I was around him. Eventually, he warmed up to me and realized I was going to be around. I was finally able to take the muzzle off. It was nice being friends again with him. Unfortunately, I left the door open, and he accidentally got out. He then bit our next-door neighbor. We had no choice but to get rid of him after that. It was all my fault; I took full responsibility for that.

For the most part, I was happy to be back, pretty excited, really. My plan was to go to a four-year college. I don't remember the exact reason why that didn't happen. I ended up going to Truman College, a community college on the north side of Chicago, instead.

I remember starting at Truman College and just feeling so out of place there. Just sitting down in the front lobby, waiting for my class to start, not knowing anybody, felt weird. I felt like I didn't fit in. I don't know if it was because I'd been in Nigeria for years or if it was just the college thing. I was a little younger than the other freshman. At seventeen, I was one of a handful of students making up the freshman class. As a result, I felt like I was out of place a lot.

Once I started to make friends, it wasn't so bad. The Community College usually had a lot of older people going there. At the time, my mom worked at *Charter One Bank*. A couple of doors down from her job was a *Subway*. She helped me get a part-time job making *Subway* sandwiches. It wasn't bad for my first job.

There was a time when I was seventeen or eighteen; I got arrested for riding my bike on the sidewalk. My brother and I were with a couple of friends, just hanging out. I believe it was only my brother and I that were on bikes; our friends were walking as we rode. We didn't go fast; we just stayed close to their walking speed. Out of the blue, the police pulled up. This was when we lived on the Northside by Lakeshore Drive.

These officers took me off my bike and put handcuffs on me! They then took me to jail! Why they took me to jail was the most ridiculous thing I had ever heard! I wasn't allowed to ride my bike on the sidewalk! This was an actual law, they said! I was dumbfounded!

My mother had to come to get me from the police station. I felt terrible she had to do that! Especially over something so ridiculous! I never had to go to court or pay a fine, so I don't know what the reason for the arrest could have been if not because of my race.

I looked it up to see if it was an actual law, and to my surprise, it is! Who knew? Do I think I would have been put in handcuffs and taken to jail if I had been white? No, I don't. If I'd been white, they would have given me a warning and told me never to do it again.

I was arrested because of the color of my skin! I had seen others ride bikes on the sidewalk. I didn't pay attention to their skin color, but then I wasn't a racist copout to cause a young black boy trouble. To this day, I have never heard of another person, be they white or black or brown, arrested for riding their bike on the sidewalk. I wouldn't be surprised if I was the only person in Chicago history to be arrested for that.

When I was at Truman, I ended up switching my major from science to business about a year in. I thought it would help me better in life once I was definite about what I wanted to do. At the time, there was a Latin street gang in my neighborhood that I got really cool with.

One of them was my next-door neighbor. We would hang out with them at times, go to their parties, and we just got really familiar with the gang in our neighborhood, the Latin Eagles. Gangs aren't all about shooting people or robbing banks, or selling drugs like portrayed in movies. I'm not saying that doesn't happen; I'm sure it does. But the Latin Eagles never once tried to recruit me. We just had mutual respect for each other and went about our lives.

I had this idea of throwing high school parties. This kid from my brother's school and I went in on this idea together. There was this older Nigerian lady that owned a restaurant that was a pretty big-sized restaurant. There was an upstairs and a downstairs that had a pretty big floor. We were able to rent it out from her for a night. We hired security, armed security—off-duty cops.

We promoted it at school, not only at my brother's high school but others in the area as well. We charged the students at the door. Security checked everybody as they entered. The only problem was at the end of the night, gang members, not the Latin Eagles, started shit. That was the first and the last party that I promoted and hosted. Too bad, really, as it was a lucrative endeavor.

My brother and I finished school. I graduated from Truman with an Associate in Arts, and my brother graduated from Lake View High School at the same time. We both chose Quincy University to go to.

Right after I graduated from Truman, before I went off to Quincy, I got in trouble with the police again. This time was for kids getting stabbed. Some kid from another high school came to our neighborhood and was causing trouble or something. The Latin Eagles in my neighborhood were called to come and intervene or talk to the kid to have him back down. I don't know why exactly, but they asked me to talk to the kid. I guess it was because the kid was black. I'm sure if the kid had been Hispanic, they probably would have taken care of it themselves, but because the kid was black, they had me come talk to him.

I spoke to him and was trying to defuse the situation when he decided to light a cigarette and blow the smoke in my face. I couldn't let something like that go. What the hell was his problem? I had to start fighting the kid.

Once I started fighting the kid showing him what a bad idea it had been to blow smoke in my face, three of the Latin Eagles jumped in and started beating on the kid as well. As I mentioned, we were friends. It escalated quickly, and then one of the gang members stabbed the kid.

I found out that the police were looking for me. I ended up getting in trouble for that a couple of days later with the police. My mom got a lawyer, and I turned myself into the police station. My mother had to pay a $10,000 bond to get me out. I was out on bond when I was able to go to Quincy. For about a year, I had to go back and forth from Quincy for court dates. At first, there was a judge that wanted me to get some jail time.

Then by the grace of God, something happened, and that judge got sick, and another judge took over. Thankfully he thought I would be good with probation as I was in school. He didn't think ruining my life would be the way to go, so he granted me probation for two years. I didn't realize it at the time, but my lawyer tricked me into signing over to him the full $10,000 bail my mother used to bond me out. She was very unhappy about that.

I went back to Quincy. My brother and I met a couple of football players there that we got really close to. My brother and I called ourselves the money team. We got jobs on campus at the cafeteria because we would run out of the meals that were provided to us by the school.

Once you run out of meals, you pretty much have to figure out how to eat on your own. Once we started working at the cafeteria, we were able to eat for free and even take food home.

My brother and I loved going to campus parties, which were at houses rented to people that went to the school. There was this one house that we went to parties at all the time called the Plantation House. Quincy was about 40,000 people. The school and the town were mostly white.

Even though the school was segregated, when it came to who hung out with who, the white kids would usually stay to themselves, and the black kids would stay to themselves. Within the groups, the football kids stayed to themselves, basketball kids to themselves, volleyball girls and guys to themselves, and so on. It was tough sometimes, especially in the dorm I stayed in. It was a single-room dorm. There was one small window. I could leave anytime I wanted, but it just felt lonely.

My most memorable time at Quincy was when a kid had Icy Hot put on his face. It was horrible. The poor kid was in so much pain, not just from the icy heat but from the embarrassment of it. We tried to find out who did it, but no one would admit to it. At one point, we were all accused, hoping that the guilty party would step forward, but no one did. That poor kid.

We were well-liked at the school. I guess that's why they thought accusing us would get a confession out of someone. It didn't work that way. It was during this horrible event Bola and I met someone we would come to learn a lot from. Quincy is a Catholic school with a disciplinary board of church members, one of which was Father Ferd. The disciplinary board that investigated the incident found that my brother and I had not been responsible.

Frier Furd became Bishop Furd in New Orleans. He recently passed. We were friends to this day; his loss is heartbreaking. He was one we could count on when we needed advice. He was always there to counsel us in any matter. His words of encouragement and faith touched so many lives, not just ours.

We got summer jobs enabling us to stay on campus over the summer to train. During the three years, I was at Quincy, Bola, and I stayed there during the summer, cutting grass and doing whatever we had to do outside. It was super hot! Super, super hot working outside every day! Not as hot as Nigeria had been, but still, it was hot!

Right after we finished working, we would go and have football practice during the afternoon and evening time. My brother and I, including other black students who worked the grounds, began to notice the easygoing jobs the white students had been given.

While we were working grounds, we'd see other kids, other *white* kids that were volleyball players and stuff, who stayed over the summer as well. They pretty much were chilling, just driving around in carts to different buildings. Doing the easiest jobs there were. It was my last year. I said, "No, we're not doing this anymore!" My brother and I called it out and made complaints, so they ended up switching us over to working inside the buildings doing stuff to shut us up.

During my last season playing football there, I got a concussion about halfway through the season and had to sit out the rest of the season. I started my football career with the Quincy Hawks in 2011. The next year, I was a linebacker for the team. My senior year, I played in three games and had one solo tackle as the Hawks's running back.

One of my fellow teammates had a studio in his room. I was interested in music and used his room to record seven songs. The music I made everyone in the school really liked. Everybody was playing my music.

With all I experienced in my final years of schooling, not once did I ever think I wished I were back in Nigeria. I'm not saying Nigeria isn't a great place. Or that the school system is less than in America. There are things about both countries that are amazing and some that aren't. Nigeria is not an easy place to be if you don't have money. If you have money in that country, you'll have the time of your life. Having no money over there, you're going to suffer. We didn't have the most money, but we weren't poor either.

I was at the stage of life where I began to make money for myself. I was able to buy things I wanted. I was pretty much-taking care of myself but was still living under my mother's roof. I had gotten my driver's license shortly after coming back to America, maybe a year after.

It wasn't hard for me to do so even though I had been in Nigeria. I was pretty much a natural when it came to driving and the driving test. My dad took me to an auction to buy a car. My first car was a Volkswagen Passat. I was very excited and happy about the car. It was my first car, so I had to pimp it out. I saved my money and bought speakers and a radio. I really pimped that car out!

I ended up crashing that vehicle. It was a snowy day, and I slid crashing into a ditch. I got it fixed, but it was never the same after that. The transmission ended up going out. I kind of miss it.

Chapter Eight

WHAT'S UPPPP?

Bola: Upon my arrival back in the States, I moved back in with my mother. After two years in Nigeria, I was looking forward to hanging out with my friends. She was now living on the north side of the Lakeview neighborhood. We had been living in Southside before Nigeria, and I was hoping to go back there. That wasn't my choice to make. As I mentioned, I had to start afresh at Lake View High. I had to make new friends and meet new people.

I can deal with people laughing at my accent, even my looks, though I don't know why they would. But my name is a different story.

I was made fun of so much that I began telling everyone my name was Jeremiah as that is my given name. I was tired of the taunting and mispronouncing of my name.

Looking back, I should have ignored the haters and continued going by Bola. That is the name I chose to go by! That is my name!

I had a few friends in high school, but they were a grade above. One of them was another African. He was more American. The other two were twins, Camel and Jamel. These were my three friends in high school.

In my freshman year, I got into my first fight in my homeroom class. I was arguing with this guy, debating, I guess, on how many bones a baby has. He said 206 bones and an adult has 200. I told him babies have around 300 bones that are very little pieces fused together. He would say no, no, no, it's not, blah blah blah. We were arguing back and forth when the bell rang.

We walk outside, and he grabs me and throws me up against the wall. I saw red! I told him to get his hands off of me! He didn't release me. Then he shouted in my face! In my face! That's what triggered me! He screamed loudly at me, saying I told you to stop talking! There are people around, and people are looking at us, so now you're making me look funny.

That's where we had the problem. He didn't leave me alone. I warned him. That's why I had to beat him up. I gave him a chance when I warned him to back off. He chose not to listen. Teachers came and separated us. I was suspended for three days. That was my first time getting suspended in high school. I know I got suspended a few times after that, but not too many. Most likely for fighting someone else who didn't heed my warning. I found out later that I was actually right; babies have 270–300 bones.

In high school, I began playing sports. My freshman year was my busiest. The soccer team was the first I auditioned for. It was a natural transition as I'd played in Nigeria.

That Icy Hot incident, my brother mentioned happened while we were at Quincy. I was on the soccer team. I had my jersey and all the required stuff, and then out of the blue, I found myself kicked off the team. The disciplinary panel asked me what teams I was associated with, and me being naive, thought that it was going to help me out, that they were trying to see what type of person I was like; I told them, I was on the soccer team, the football team, I run track. I think this is going to show them I am not a bad person, that I am a team player. That I didn't do this cruel prank, they were investigating. Boy, was I wrong!

The next time I went to soccer practice, I was told I wouldn't be a good addition to the team. By this time, I'd been thinking about leaving the team anyway. I'd scored a goal at practice, which wasn't easy to do, yet the coach left me on the bench! Then to hear I wasn't a good fit for the team was like a slap in the face!

I was given no explanation why I suddenly didn't "fit in" with a team. I was the only black person on the team. My skills were better than a few of the others. Yet the coach wouldn't put me in! The team was fairly decent. I never felt like a part of it, anyway. I'm not going to lie; I was hurt by the casual way I was dropped from the team. I dreamed of playing soccer when I left that team; I left that dream.

I put all of my energy into track and football. That soccer coach didn't realize what he had! My track and football coaches both knew what a bonus I was to the teams! I was very underappreciated in my high school career.

I had always been the underdog in football. I had to work my way up. In my sophomore year, I was playing defense. I was pretty good at it. My junior year was my first playing varsity. In varsity, I played defense and special teams. I've always wanted to play offense or run the ball or score the ball because I was fast. I knew I had the ability to do so. In my junior year, the coaches knew that, and when an opportunity arose when the kick returner got injured, they told me this was my time. I had repeatedly said I just needed a chance, and they had just given it to me.

The first time they put me in, I scored a touchdown off a kick. I may not have made all of them, but I made most of them. They made me the kick returner after that. Every game, when a kick return was needed, I was called in. I would score a touchdown every time. It got to the point where coaches saw films of my performances, and the teams started kicking the ball out of bounds instead of kicking it to me because they didn't want me to run it back on them. Knowing that gave me so much joy because I always knew what I was capable of, and now having my peers and coaches witness it gave me so much happiness. That was how I spent my junior and senior years.

Since they now saw that I could run and score, they began to put me in to play offense. I was a running back. That year was a great year for me, playing running back. I had so many yards! So many touchdowns! During my senior year, before the season even started, we were practicing running a play. There was a sled on the field. I was running back out for a pass, looking up.

The ball was coming down, but I hit the sled before I could catch the ball. My knee was banged up. I don't remember exactly what the doctor said, but they wanted to do an MRI. I remember the doctor had a needle to take fluid out of the knee, but that didn't work. I had to wait for the swelling to subside on its own. Eventually, it did, but it gave me more problems because I was never healed fully before I played my first game. In my second or third game, I had a high ankle sprain on the same leg putting me out for another game.

In the end, even though there were three or four other running backs, I still had the most yards and most touchdowns of the season because I was very good. Anytime I touched the ball as a running back, people were expecting something to happen. I don't think I've ever had yards for loss as a running back.

I had very good grades in school. My teachers and I got along. I really was well-liked by them. I say that a lot, but it's true. I am a very likable person. My three friends were instrumental in me being accepted. There were a few groups of other people that I ran into that they had provided a sense of protection from.

In Southside, we encountered gangs, but the ones in my high school weren't the same. My three friends were respected not just because of who their families were but because they were big guys too. After that fight my freshman year, I had a few more. People began to see that I had proven myself and that I wasn't one to back down. I wasn't going to let anyone bully me. They may start the fight, but I would end it!

In my senior year, my sister became a freshman. By this time, I was well respected throughout the school. Everyone knew who I was, but not everyone liked me. They may not like me, but they respected me. Everyone knew she was my sister, and she wasn't to be messed with. If you asked my sister, she would tell you my legacy remained even after I graduated.

No one was brave enough to dare go after her in any way. Only three years prior, I had been a newbie in my freshman year. I graduated, having transformed myself into a well-respected member of the student body. I had proven that not only was I a great football player and an amazing track star but also a guy that had earned the respect of my peers. I made my mark at that school.

A defensive coach, and a recruiter, came to Lake View High to check out any possible players. My head coach at Lake View pulled three of us aside and told us the recruiter/coach wanted to talk to us. He offered us a chance to come to Quincy to check out the school. That is what recruiters do. We went on a tour, and two of us, me and a guy named Rafael, decided Quincy was the school for us. The third one couldn't afford to as Quincy was super expensive, almost $40,000 a year, I believe. Within the first year, Raphael ended up dropping out due to tuition being too high.

I had an academic scholarship because of my grades at Lake View High School. Quincy helped me out a lot. Even though a coach/recruiter had first suggested Quincy because of the sports I did, the scholarship money was purely academic. I didn't receive any sports scholarship like I thought I would. The coach had told me that he thought I would get at least one scholarship for sports, but he was wrong. Track was one of the sports that I had proved myself in. It was never a problem for me. Running was something I'd always been good at. I loved doing track! Then I tore my hamstring. It healed, but I didn't race any more that year. The year after, I thankfully didn't pull it again. I made it all the way through college and then in March of 2021, I pulled it right before a boxing match at a national tournament. What can I say? I am good at what I do, even if it is pulling a hamstring!

In college, my brother and I had the same group of friends. Usually, I befriend older people. I've never really been close to my peers. I just naturally gravitate to older people. I remember this time in college that was quite significant to me. In my Earth Science class, my classmates and I were playing bingo or jackpot, where you work in teams, and you had to figure out the answer.

We were talking amongst ourselves, and I noticed that when I would say an answer, they would look at me. It was like they saw and heard me but also like I wasn't there. Sort of like I didn't exist. Like what I was saying didn't matter. Talk about getting mad... I was like, what the hell? It wasn't like the answer I said was wrong! I knew the answer! Science is my thing! And suddenly, I am invisible. I don't think so! I loved science. The thing is, I knew the answer. Like I said, I was smart.

They ignored me, and when they had to give the answer, they gave the wrong one. I was right! The look they gave me after that was like it was a fluke; I had been right like they didn't believe it would happen again. After once more, giving them a correct answer, and my classmates would ignore me and say the wrong answer, only to see, I was right, I stopped answering. Evidently, the rest of the people in my group didn't mind losing! I found myself thinking to myself, did they really see me as someone inferior who didn't know anything because of the color of my skin? I was the only black person in that class.

Was it racism? It had to be. I wasn't the only male on the team. It was made up of males and females. If it wasn't because of the color of my skin, why not give the answer I said? Even if I'd been wrong, if they had just once used what I said, I wouldn't have thought this way. But blatantly ignoring the answer I offered and then looking shocked I was right had to be a form of racism.

Was it because of the color of my skin they didn't want to take a chance on the answer because they thought I couldn't possibly know the answer? Why didn't my opinion matter? They lost because they wouldn't trust a black man!

Sadly, this wasn't a one-time thing. This continued to happen throughout my college career, really through all my educational experience. There were people, not just students but teachers as well, throughout high school and college that seemed to think I wasn't smart because of the color of my skin! This was one reason I had a chip on my shoulder! I was on the Dean's list all the time and graduated in the Honors program! I showed them you can't judge how smart someone is by the color of their skin! I graduated feeling good about that!

Chapter Nine

COLLEGE VIBES

Ola: I am thankful for the opportunity to see and experience school in both America and Nigeria. I truly believe the time I had in Nigeria at school helped to make me stronger and able to face more in my academic career in America! Nigeria's curriculum is different from America's. I wasn't taught the same things.

Bola: There were a few things I missed out on in Nigeria that were taught here, like how to divide fractions. That's not that big of a thing, and it's not something you would use every day. Microsoft Excel, however, was something that I hadn't learned and needed to know. I was in high school, seeing everyone around me knew how to do that, but I just looked confused.

Sometimes I would ask the teacher to explain it, but there were thirty people in the classroom, they either didn't want to or they didn't want to just stop and explain. I was kind of shy, and with the accent, I was hesitant to put myself under scrutiny. I didn't want to seem dumb; I wasn't. It was just something that I wasn't taught in school while in Nigeria.

It wasn't like I didn't learn as fast as the other students in the class; I did. It was that some things weren't taught in Nigeria, so I was just learning something they had learned about prior to that class. There were times in class when I would be like damn, I understand none of that shit. I wanted to understand it! It's not like I wasn't paying attention; I was.

In America, we had every subject every day, so I couldn't even focus on one subject. I had to move on to the next one. Once I left that class, that's it. I'm not thinking about it anymore. I'm thinking about the next class. Nigeria prepared me to work hard, but I missed out on classes taught in America that I would need in life.

My social life at Quincy was infused with my brother's. We had the same friends. Even though my brother and I were cleared by the investigation board on that kid's Icy Hot incident. I was suddenly a threat to society! It didn't matter that I'd been cleared of any wrongdoing. I found myself removed from the room I shared in one dorm room to a private dorm. They thought they were punishing me, but it was to my satisfaction because I now had room to myself. I was very happy with that.

I was kind of antisocial. I spent a lot of my time in that room. I now had time by myself. Sometimes I just like escaping and being alone. I bought speakers, and at times I would play loud music while chilling or practicing different things I watched from videos online. I may have been put in my own room as some kind of punishment, but I took full advantage of it.

As a defensive back for the Quincy Hawks, I was on my path to being an NFL player. In 2012 I played in eleven games as a defensive back. I recorded twenty tackles and forced one fumble of the season. I was named Great Lake Valley Conference Academic All-Conference. In 2013, I played in all eleven games and recorded thirty-three tackles. I had 2.5 tackles for a loss. I recovered two fumbles, returning one for a touchdown against Kentucky Wesleyan College.

I am an easy-going guy. As long as I'm treated with respect, I will do the same. I don't remember what the fallout was, but if it meant leaving the team, I would do so. Unfortunately, this time it interfered with my NFL plans. Was this a sign that football wasn't my path after all?

I also was acting at this time. I had done a few plays while in high school with an after-school program called After School Matters. I was a part of a production. I played the main villain in the production. My name was Tek. I altered my voice. It was a very difficult thing to do, but

I would alter my voice. Since it was so difficult, I was the only character in the play that used the microphone as it was very difficult for me to project my voice.

I did many plays in college as well. I was part of the theater division. I majored in biology and theater in college. I passed most of my subjects with flying colors. The most difficult subject I had was physics. There were some things I knew that others didn't, and vice versa. I was thrilled to get out of that class!

I've always liked science. When it came time to choose my major, it seemed like going into a major that required science was a good idea. I like science, but I was good at any subject really, even the ones that were somewhat difficult, like math. But I was good at it. The math teacher asked me to be a math major. My English teacher asked me to be an English major. Each teacher I had wanted me to major in what they taught. I could have done that, but my first love won out.

I chose science though not why you'd think. It was my hate for writing. I hate it! I was a good writer in my English class, but I couldn't imagine going into a field that required doing that all the time! I chose the subject I thought would have the least amount of writing. I thought biology would be that, but low and behold, I had to write lab reports. That just sucked! And now my brother and I are writing this book!

I also majored in theater; at least I wasn't required to write that much in it! When we were younger, my mother saw one of those commercials talking about an open casting call for Disney or something like that for any show. My mom took me, Ola, and my two sisters to audition. They only selected me.

I've always had a passion for acting or theater. That's why I acted in college. My teacher, Connie Phillips, was instrumental in my stay at Quincy. She was like a mother to me at Quincy. She showed a lot of love to me. Helping me out. We always had deep conversations. I feel I learned a lot from her about theater and life.

I worked on the grounds with Ola doing the grounds and maintenance work over the summer, so we had some money. The food arrangements were difficult at Quincy. There was only a certain number of meals allotted a year for the meal plan, and I had money on my Flex card.

I would run out of meals and cash. I was able to deal with that better than some of the other students, as I had run out when I was in boarding school. I never told my parents about this, not until later on. If I did, they might have given me more money.

The dating scene was difficult. I am a hot commodity, as you can see in all my pictures in this book. It was tough. How was I to have the social life I wanted on the small amount of cash I had? Many people wouldn't look my way. I knew why; a lot of those people who went to Quincy University come from small towns. They're not used to black people. Some of them are not attracted to black people and stick to what they know. I was like, damn, am I not attractive? What's going on? A lot of people were just scared to go out of their comfort zone. It got easier later on, in my junior and senior years.

Ola: It got so desperate that we would even have to go off campus. There was online dating at the time, but that didn't work for us. Women were a challenge at the time, but we found ways to date, even on our meager funds. The women were in full supply; it was just hard getting one to say yes. As Bola mentioned, they had their reasons to say no.

Bola: There were a few issues after we were accused of the Icy Hot incident with girls, but we moved passed that when exonerated. The only good thing that came out of that debacle was Frier Furd. He took us on two mission trips with him, one to Biloxi, Mississippi, and the second to New Orleans after Hurricane Katrina. We helped plant trees, put new light bulbs in older people's houses, and helped clean their houses. We even helped nuns out at a convent. Growing up, our parents instilled in all of us that helping a friend, being there to listen to a friend no matter the reason, was the right thing to do. This is something I try to do to this day.

During one of these mission trips, we had the opportunity to experience Mardi Gras for the first time, but some of those people are crazy! The things I saw… I think some of my fellow students forgot why we were there. They not only went to a strip club which was bad enough, but they filmed it! If you go to a Catholic school and then are dumb enough to film yourself at a strip club, whatever your punishment is, it is no one's fault but your own!

That wasn't even the craziest thing! They accused Ola of being there too! They said they saw him there! Though he wasn't in the video. The only thing that saved Ola was that he and I were with a few other friends at the time, playing cards with Frier Furd. People were always quick to throw us into the mix, trying to get us in trouble. I don't know if they were jealous of us or just the vindictive kind.

Those students couldn't figure out how they were found out. This is the digital age! There is always someone with a phone, usually more than one person. At least one of them decided to video them in a strip club which was bad enough! But one of them thought posting it on social media was a good idea! From there, it was shared, and there was no way they could delete it. I don't think the school punished them other than sending them home. I'm thankful Ola was with me and the Frier.

Ola: We got really close to the president of the school Quincy University and his wife. They invited us over for dinner once as well. Bola may not be one for authority, but we were always close to those in charge.

Bola: There was this one time my senior year in college I was chosen by a group called CEO, a mastermind business group, to go to Disneyland, and the school would pay for it. I was the only student who got to go with a teacher as a chaperone.

Ola: After I graduated from Quincy in 2014 with my business management degree, I learned how to behave professionally as well as conduct myself as a college graduate going forth into the world to forge my own path.

Bola: After being in my own dorm room, I reluctantly left it behind my sophomore year. I moved into the same dorm room with Ola and his roommate, Pre in my junior year, I shared their room too. The S.L.C. (Student Living Center) was the newest dorm on campus.

Pre and I started a group we called Team Abel. We were hoping it would get us more chicks. But that wasn't the only reason. We wanted to show off our physique, our body. We would practice our backflips and calisthenics. The name Team Abel was obvious because he and I were a team. It was also a play on words. Cain and Abel, Abel being the good brother and us representing that.

Ola: I joined Team Abel with them. During the time I was getting my master's degree, I studied finance. I went back to Quincy to visit my brother and hung out with everybody. We were good friends, not to mention I was into calisthenics too. When Bola graduated from Quincy, we started a party supply store called Party Time. Our mother thought it would be a good business for us. I think we kept that open for about two years before we closed it, around 2017.

I graduated from Keller in 2017. My time there was nothing like the other schools I'd been to. I guess because I was older, and I didn't stay on campus. I went home each day and then went to my security job. I was security at a restaurant called Cheesie's Pub and Grub. They sold different types of grilled cheese sandwiches. Who knew there could be so many kinds? They were good too!

Right next to them was a gay nightclub called Berlin, where I was a bouncer. There were transgender individuals, transgender prostitutes, that would walk by. They walked up and down and almost always caused trouble and started fights.

It was one of those things you saw but didn't see. As long as they didn't cause trouble for us, I left them alone. They knew who I was and would say hi when they walked by. They knew I wouldn't let them get by with causing trouble on my watch! They got into criminal activity and began to rob people, but that didn't happen on my watch or in the club I was bouncing for. I stayed out of their way, and they stayed out of mine.

Since I didn't live on campus at that time, I went back and forth to school from there. I breezed through the classes I needed for my master's degree. It was the easiest of the three for me out of all my associate's and bachelor's. My masters were by far the easiest for me. My GPA was 3.7. At Quincy, it was a 3.0. I don't remember what the other one was.

Bola: School wasn't really hard on me. I got my bachelor's, and everyone said I should push on and get my master's to help further my career, but quite frankly, I hated school! I hate school with a passion!

Even though I hated school, I was good at it. Not just the academic part of it but the social part as well. Looking back, I can see I relied on my charm a lot. I was quite the charmer when I needed to be. If I'd been able to go through school on my charm alone, I might have gone on to school to get my other degrees, but the studying part I burned out on.

My parents would have liked to see me go on, but it wasn't right for me. I knew that and could see no reason to push forward when I wouldn't need another degree for the goals in my life. They understood that.

Team Abel Logo

Chapter Ten

CASTING CALL

Bola: I graduated from college and moved back with my parents and Ola on the Northside. Chris moved in with us. We decided it was time to open an Instagram account for Team Abel and began making it into a brand. We were going to do cool fitness stunts and activities. We wanted to do classes in Chicago for children, but we never got into it. We maintained doing the fitness stunts and signing up for aerobatic classes where we do backflips, front flips, and all. The place was called Chair Destiny.

We joined a dance group where we put on maybe three shows. The group was called Body Moving Dance. The group consisted of three guys and ten girls. We three guys were mostly props for the girls. It wasn't too long before that ended, but the girls were amazing! It was great working with them. That experience added to my theatrical endeavors.

In 2015, we were looking into getting into the acting world. My mom saw there was a movie being filmed in Chicago. Knowing my brother and I were looking into acting, she told us where it was and we went to check it out. Being naive, not knowing how the game worked, we went in thinking once they saw us, we would be hired. We were attractive guys with a distinct look. Why wouldn't they choose us to act in the movie or TV show?

The movie was *Chi-Raq* by Spike Lee. Spike Lee! The man is legendary! His movies are amazing! I had no idea what the film was about, but I knew I wanted to be in it!

We didn't know how these things worked. We talked to the first person we encountered. I think she was a production assistant. We were told that wasn't the way things were done. Turns out you don't just show up and get cast. She told us about a website we needed to sign up on. The casting director would then decide if they wanted to cast you.

My brother, Chris, and I all signed up. I was cast to play a national guard extra. Pre and I got the similar roles. Spike Lee wanted a few of the extras to try out for roles with dancing. If I was chosen, this could change my life! I danced for him, hoping to be bumped from an extra to a principal performer. Chris danced as well.

Spike Lee handpicked me! Me! And Chris. Suddenly I had numerous 'cameos' in films. One scene put me dead center in a scene. There was no way I would be missed! I felt like I was finally living my destiny! This was the first step on the path of my journey to where I needed to be, where I was meant to be. The doors were opened wide for me, with no resistance.

Ola was cast on a new TV show called Empire. I had hoped we would all be cast in the movie. It would have been cool being on screen together.

We used Four-Star Casting to sign up officially to book more extra roles. I was cast on a number of Chicago-based shows. I was an extra in *Chicago PD* a few times before finally getting a speaking role. *Chicago PD* was my first speaking role for a big production.

Around 2015, I landed a role on a new show about a feuding divorced couple and the legacy of the multimillion-dollar company *Empire*. Ola had been an extra on the series by this point. I had been on the show for a while by this time as an extra. I was handpicked by *Empire's* executive producer, Sanaa Hamri. She picked me because she liked my look.

As an extra, you had to bring your own clothes and have two or three different outfits. I wore my African outfits, so when she saw me, she said she liked me and asked who I was. Then she said she was going to put me right where the camera would see me.

That was a good and a bad thing. The bad thing was not being able to go on any more auditions because you were already on camera. The good thing is I was selected. She now knows who I am, she noticed me, and she has a lot to say about who was on the show and if they had a speaking role or were just a little face in the background. She also directed a few episodes. I was happy to have the role. Every time I was there, she would position me in a great location, so I was in a great position to be on camera. I was being seen!

After a while, she gave me a title: Head of World Music. I was in the A&R Department. I felt special as this was a step in the direction I wanted my life to go. Any office scenes, which were in every episode, I was in it. I was a part of the core group. I would spend four to five times a week on filming. The money was consistent, and I was around the star power actors. Those that were household names were Taraji B Henson. Terrence Howard. Chris Rock and Jussie Smollett, to name a few. I used my time on set, watching how they prepared for their part. Their acting was a learning experience for me.

I was an extra on a few episodes of *Chicago PD*, but mainly I was on *Empire.* In 2018, with Jussie's help, I became a stand-in for his love interest on *Empire.* One day he hit me up. He was like, "Hey, do you want to be a stand-in?"

I said, "Hell yeah, I wanna be a stand-in." A stand-in is used for rehearsals, camera blocking, and lighting setups instead of the principal actor. Stand-ins get paid more and are treated like they are an actor. My paycheck significantly increased. Much more so than a background actor. You get to eat with the actors and the production team and crew. You are treated better as a stand-in. It was a big upgrade, of course, and I wanted to stay a stand-in! The hell with being the head of the music world.

The only downside of being a stand-in is you're not seen on camera. I thought that was cool because I really wanted to act. I was a real actor, even if I was only a stand-in. I didn't want to be just a cameo with a few lines. I wanted to be a supporting actor on my way to being a lead actor. I had already been an extra, and now I was a stand-in. The next stop would be supporting actors on my road to success. I was a stand-in actor up until 2019, until the incident with Jussie.

Everything changed! Once I had a speaking role, no matter how small, I was able to call myself a professional actor. The experience was a great way to see how the difference in your place amongst the actors on a small show or a movie. Sadly, whatever level of actor you are dictates how you are treated and how you treat others on set. Being around those actors, a bond forms from working on a scene and then multiple takes.

The experience of being an extra and then having speaking lines in a more prominent character was fun to me. They all felt natural to me. I didn't feel any kind of pressure in the role I did to be better than anyone else. Mostly I was playing a second-in-command sort of role, as I wasn't able to be picky. There aren't that many opportunities for shows filming in Chicago compared to Los Angeles.

In 2016 or 2017, a friend recommended I audition for a role in an independent movie being shot for *Amazon Prime: Friends, Family, and Lovers.* I wasn't reading for the main character. I read for a smaller role. I am very confident in my acting ability and always believe that I can be the lead. I read whatever role they gave me. Not knowing which one was the lead. I did my audition in my Nigerian accent; the director/producer liked my audition and had me read for another character at the time. I didn't know it was for the main character. He changed his script to give the main character an African accent because he liked me for the part.

The movie was about two friends; one was a deadbeat with baby mama drama, and the other was constantly helping him out. He finds someone he believes loves him and wants to settle down. A comedy of errors happens, and then… Did you really think I would tell you how the movie ends? You'll just have to watch it to find out!

I then did another movie, The Worst Nightmare. It was about a music producer who steals a friend's music and claims it as his own. The guy gets arrested for something he didn't do. Ola was in this film too.

It had the potential to be a great movie, but it had no production behind it.

It was another step toward my destiny.

After graduation, I did a few plays. As Ola mentioned, our mother thought a party supply store was a good idea for us. We tried, it failed, and we moved on.

Ola: After I got my masters in 2017, I went back to Quincy University to act in a play. The play was about the underground railroad. Quincy, Illinois was the first underground railroad station across from Missouri, a slave state. We played Slaves escaping slavery and Dr. Richard Eells helping us escape. The play was actually performed in the still-standing home of Dr. Richard Eells in Quincy Illinois.

As he said, I was cast on *Empire* while Bola and Chris were working with Spike Lee. It would have been so cool to work with a legend like Spike Lee, but that time will come. But it's all good. *Empire* was the work of Lee Daniels! The man is a legend! I started as an extra, but the lead director took a liking to me and handpicked me to upgrade my role to a feature. I was upgraded to a feature role. I was chosen to be Chris Rock's—one of the stars of the show–bodyguard. Lee Daniels took a picture with me and Matt Hearston on the set of the show and posted it to his Instagram. My first time being on set, and I was already on the amazing Lee Daniels Instagram!

Many would say this was just the luck of the draw. Or being in the right place at the right time. I would disagree with that. There is some kind of energy that draws people to me, to my brother. That is why the doors were opening for us. This was the plan the Almighty had for us.

In 2016, I signed on with Babes and Beaus Talent Agency. I began auditioning for different roles through them. I just wanted to see if they could help me as I journeyed toward my destiny. I landed a guest starring role in *Chicago PD* in 2017.

Chapter Eleven

MUSCLE UP

Ola: In 2017 Bola and I went to a fitness convention in Rosemont, Illinois, a suburb of Chicago. I was doing calisthenics. This is something Bola, and I enjoyed doing. Calisthenics is an amazing way to exercise, as well as benefits my health. I was making a move I had done thousands of times before, but this time I put my hands in a different position. As a result, I tore my bicep muscle from my elbow. I had to wait six months before I could have surgery on it.

Bola: I won best abs and best back. At the time I wasn't into bodybuilding. That came later. I became interested in professional bodybuilding. I went on to participate in natural bodybuilding which is for bodybuilders who don't use performance-enhancing drugs to enhance their physique.

In the first leg of the event, I had to do a lie detector test and a urine test. I expected to win that show as I expect to win every show. When we do things, it is to be the best. We never do it just to do it. My brother and I never fear to excel. We are confident in everything we do. I won every show that I did and got my pro card after winning the first bodybuilding show I did.

My 5th show was with a different league, a different federation. This show was called the Natural Olympia by the PNBA Federation. I placed fifth. However, I was the best-looking person physique-wise in the show.

But because of politics, I got fifth. I talked to a judge that told me it would be because I was from a different federation, and they couldn't let someone who came from a different federation take first at a federation where no one knew me.

Not to mention it would look bad on the federation if I came from another federation and immediately won. That just put a bad taste in my mouth. I didn't like losing. But losing for such a ridiculous reason really put me off.

I worked very hard and put myself through so much stress. Getting ready for a show like that requires mental, physical, and spiritual preparation. You have to put yourself in completely, 100% if you do something like that. If you want to compete in something like that, you have to push yourself to the limits, to the point you feel like you're falling. After putting so much into being the best you and then being told by a judge you should have won is like a slap in the face. Did he really think I would be happy with fifth place after that?

I had a decision to make, did I continue along this path or move on to something that would once more lead me to my destiny? I knew I didn't want to participate, to continue on with a sport where I would be cheated as I'd been with bodybuilding. I had thought about boxing before.

A few days after my bodybuilding show, a friend from high school called. I called him the African back then. It had been a while since I talked to him. Then, not two days later, he randomly called me, and after we talked for a while, he asked me why I didn't get into boxing. He knew I had fought in high school. That was a divine confirmation from the Almighty.

There was no way that was a coincidence. Boxing was the next step toward my future. My last bodybuilding show was on November 11th, 2018. My first boxing event took place on December 6, 2018. I won that fight. I knocked my opponent out of the ring the same way I knocked bodybuilding from my life! When my opponent went out of the ring, I knew a boxing career was going to be the best thing for me.

Chapter Twelve

JUSSIE WHO?

Bola: I met Jussie in 2016. A mutual friend invited me to Jussie's house. We were talking one day, and he said, 'Hey, you wanna go to Jussie's house?' I said, 'Yeah, I'll go.' That friend and I went to Jussie's crib. I think my friend was going to drop off some weed to a friend that just happened to be at Jussie's house. We chilled a little bit and watched some TV while they smoked. This was the first time I hung out with Jussie. I didn't get his contact information until the second or third time I hung out with him and our mutual friend. We were forming a friendship, Jussie and I.

My friend Jussie and I would go clubbing. We'd go for dinner or drinks. There was an occasional party or just chilling at his house. Eventually, Jussie asked me to help get him some weed and Molly. So, I did. Eventually, he asked me to be his love interest's stand-in.

As I mentioned before, I agreed. Jussie asked me if I was comfortable playing a gay character. I wasn't expecting that. At the time, I didn't know why he was asking. I answered him truthfully. I told him I didn't know if I'd be comfortable doing that on TV.

After telling him I'd love to be the stand-in, Jussie told me he'd get back to me. Thinking back, I think he asked me those questions because he wanted me to play his love interest on the show, but I didn't feel comfortable doing that.

I agreed to only be a stand-in for Kai, the character in love with Jussie. The funny thing is the actor who played Kai was a Nigerian as well. Jussie and I hung out a few times. Later on in our friendship, my friend and I went with Jussie to a bathhouse. I had no idea what a bathhouse was. I quickly found out. A bathhouse is where gay and bisexual men can spend time together in various ways.

When I got there, I was astounded at what I saw going on. I was a little taken aback, and I was a little frightened because it was dark in there. The men there looked mad at the world. Definitely gave off a scary vibe. Some of the men were walking around naked. You are given a locker for your stuff and a room. You can put all kinds of stuff in a room.

The first time we were there, I chilled in the sauna or the hot tub. Occasionally I'd go to the weight room. I usually hung out there while waiting for Jussie. It was a clean, well-equipped weight room. It looked as if no one used it. As we walked through, some of the room doors were open. As we walked by, the people were doing various things. There was a one-time Jussie went into of the rooms.

My friend and I just kept walking. I went there three times with Jussie. Looking back on things now, I see he had ulterior motives for taking me there. He knew I wasn't interested in any kind of relationship with him. Taking me to a bathhouse hoping I may change my mind would be pointless. Did he take me there for shock value? I'm a grown man, there isn't anything that could shock me there. Having had time to think it over, I know he was taking me there as a way to groom me. He wanted to turn me into the kind of actor he wanted me to be. He was taking me to the bathhouse to see if I would be more comfortable engaging in homosexual activities.

January 20th, 2019, Jussie asked me to make him a meal plan and workout program because he had a music video shoot coming up in February. I asked if he had any dietary restrictions before creating a platform. I sent it to him.

January 24, 2019, at 9:34 AM, he texted.

Jussie: I might need your help on the low you around to meet up and talk face to face later, like 4.

Bola: I could.

Around two, he asked where I was.

Bola: I was at the gym finishing up.

Jussie: Where? It'll take like 20 minutes.

I told him where the gym was, and he asked me how far from the stage the gym was.

Bola: 30 minutes.

Jussie: Can we meet? Can you meet me there? We can ride and talk.

Bola: Yeah, I can.

Jussie: Cool.

Eventually, I texted him at 3:23, telling him I was there.

He had me come outside to the breezeway. About ten minutes later, we were riding around. At first, we were just talking about nothing in particular. A week earlier, he showed me a letter that had been sent to the studio threatening him. He wanted to talk about how the studio wasn't taking it seriously. I could tell he was aggravated that they didn't see the possible threat and want to do whatever it took to keep him safe. The letter showed a stick figure hanging with a gun and the words You will die, you black fag, written with letters cut from magazines. The envelope had MAGA as the return address and was addressed to the studio Center Space Studios, where *Empire* was being filmed.

The letter had been received on January 22nd with a white powder inside. The studio's reaction wasn't what Jussie thought it should be. He told me they weren't taking it seriously. He felt this matter was serious. His life had been threatened, and yet no one seemed to think he should be worried. Right after, he said he wanted me to fake attack him. At first,

I just stared at him. I had to have heard him wrong. Who says, I want you to attack me?

In my head. I was thinking he just smoked weed. He's high! He has to be high! He has to be high as hell! Jussie must have noticed the weird look on my face because he said again, "I want you to fake attack me, but we're going to set it up where you attack me. We will put it on social media for everyone to see."

Jussie didn't say if he had an agenda when he told me what he wanted. I can't speak for him, but I think he wanted to be a martyr to eventually push his political career or activism. Should he want to be an activist?

He went on to tell me he wanted me to beat him, but he also wanted me to act like he was fighting back so he would look strong. I was still having trouble believing he actually wanted me to beat him up.

Jussie told me he needed another attacker; did I think my brother would do it?

By this point, I was beginning to see he was serious. He really wanted me to fake attack him. Not only me but my brother as well. Would Ola go along with this crazy idea? I had no idea, but I told Jussie, "Hell yeah, my brother would do it! Why wouldn't he want to?"

We headed for my house as the snow fell. I don't know if Jussie still thought I was unsure about what he was asking, but he began to talk about how this was a normal thing in Hollywood. Things of this sort were orchestrated by celebrities to gain more publicity, but it has to be real, or at least appear so. He mentioned that the robbery in Paris was staged. Kim Kardashian planned the whole thing, Jussie said. After that, I thought, if this was how Hollywood did things, I'd made it! I'm going to be a part of Hollywood! Let's do this!

Let's do this! Jussie never mentioned the police in any way. That didn't cross my mind. I thought this was what Hollywood did. The police would have no place in the fake attack we were orchestrating for social media. There were the occasional moments of unease. The question of why he wanted me to do the attack was such a random statement, totally out of the blue. I told myself this might be a weird thing to ask, but once he told me there was going to be a camera that would film it all, I began to tell myself it was just another acting gig.

I found it bizarre to not only ask me but to even think of doing such a thing. Eventually, we roll back to my house. As we pulled into the alley, Ola was there. It was perfect timing. He was going to the mailbox or coming back from it. I told him to hop into the car.

Ola slid into the back seat. The middle, I think. Jussie asked him if he could trust him.

Chapter Thirteen

CAN I TRUST YOU?

Ola: I first met Jussie through my brother. I'd seen him around set, but it wasn't until Bola took me to his apartment that I actually officially met him. Then we hung out a few times and went clubbing. I had just taken the trash out, and gotten the mail when a Mercedes pulled up. The window came down to reveal my brother. He told me to hop in. I did.

Jussie asked if he could trust me. It was an odd question, but I told him he could. I'm sure he'd already asked my brother if he thought I could be trustworthy. And, of course, Bola would have said yes. Jussie proceeded to tell me about the plan, about attacking him. I heard all about the letter and the studio's lack of interest in protecting him.

My first thought upon hearing the plan was he was crazy. There was no way he was serious! He couldn't truly mean for us to attack him, fake or not! I had heard about Hollywood doing crazy things but had never been asked to be a part of it. Jussie was a member of the Inner Circle. If he said, it was done in Hollywood, who was I to argue?

This attack was supposed to go on social media. My brother and I never were never supposed to be blown up the way we were. That was the only reason I went along with it. I believed he needed our help, and we would be doing him a favor. In return, maybe he could help us out with our careers in the future.

Jussie never mentioned the police. Not once did he say the fake attack would become a real attack. Had he mentioned the police, neither Bola nor I would have agreed. In our culture, we don't like being involved with any type of police at all. We try to avoid the police as much as possible. To willingly put ourselves in harm's way would be against what we believe in.

Bola: On January 26th at 4:50 PM, Jussie texted me.

Jussie: You still down to train tomorrow?

The 27th was supposed to be the rehearsal. He was going to take us to the place and rehearse.

Jussie: Yeah, meet me at 7:15 AM.

Bola: I have a ceremony. I won't be done until 9:00 AM.

Jussie: Alright. I'm picking up my creative director Frank at 8:30 AM. Just hit me after your ceremony. I have a flight to East Coast tomorrow at 3:00 PM.

Bola: Alright, will do.

On the morning of the 27th at 9:15 AM, he texted me again.

Jussie: Where are you at?

Bola (9:22): On my way back to Chicago.

Jussie: How long?

Bola (9:31): An hour

10:53 Jussie: here.

Bola (10:56): where are you at?

I went outside looking for him.

Jussie: I'm out front.

Ola and I hopped in as Jussie drove us to the scene. Looking back, I should have had a red flag upon seeing where Jussie wanted us to 'attack' him, the 300th block of East North Water Street. That is not the part of town that you would expect would be attackers to be. Seriously, Oprah lived nearby! But not once did that thought cross my mind.

It was not far from his apartment. Jussie told us what the plan was. He said he wanted us to fake "attack" him. He wants me to fake punch him because he didn't trust Ola to pull his punch. He told me he wanted me to do it. He joked about it, then told us the materials we would need.

1. Red hats
2. Gasoline
3. Rope to make a noose

The red hats, he said, were to make the attackers look like they were Donald Trump supporters. He said we needed to make sure we said this is MAGA country. We were instructed to use racial and homophobic slurs. He said to say, 'Aren't you that nigger faggot from that Empire show? This is MAGA country!' Why was Jussie insistent we bring MAGA into it? Why the red hat and slurs involving the President?

Jussie said he would be on the phone with one of his managers. The manager wouldn't know what was going on, but he'd hear and could corroborate in case the media came to him or something. That way, if asked, he could say, oh yeah, I was on the phone when that happened. The manager wasn't aware this was a fake "attack." The manager testified that he heard what was happening, which is what Jussie had said he would want corroboration. He just failed to mention that it would be on a witness stand.

Once we were at the "attack" site, Jussie drove around it a few times before pointing out the camera. He made a point of saying that the camera would capture everything. We stayed there a while before heading back home.

When we arrived home, Jussie wrote out the check for $3500 and gave it to me. We were supposed to be paid $4000, but he said he'd give us the $500 upon our return from Nigeria. On the check, Jussie wrote. It was payment for the meal and exercise plan he had me make for him. That was just a cover for the truth.

Looking back, I can see he wrote that to say he didn't pay us to attack him when he went to the police. He knew we were going to Nigeria. That's why he wanted us to do the attack before he left. He was going to the East Coast, New York. He wanted to time it that he would be just getting back from New York, and we'd attack him.

The main reason I agreed to do the "attack" was because he was a friend. He needed my help. The other reason was he could help me. He was someone who could help me advance my acting career by giving me pointers on how to improve my skills. I enjoy learning new things that will help me to better myself.

Not to mention, Hollywood can be difficult to break into. In Hollywood, it's not who you know but who you know. Jussie could help me open doors too. Between that and all the financial stuff, clubbing, drinks, etcetera, I felt like I owed him. I was indebted to him.

With the check in hand, Jussie dropped my brother and me off at home. He gave us $100 to go buy the supplies we bought, the Red Hat, gloves, rope, mask, and hand warmers.

Ola: Jussie wanted us to use gasoline, but I said no. There are numerous reasons why gas was a bad idea. He agreed, and we changed it to bleach. I felt bleach would be something I would use at home, something that I would have on hand upon coming up with a plan to 'attack' someone. I put it in a hot sauce bottle, as that was all I could find.

Up until Jussie's planning session, I'd met him three or four times. Bola had met him more than that. I'd gone through the dry run the day before I was with Bola at the store buying the supplies. We didn't buy anything to put the bleach in, which is why I use the Tabasco bottle.

Chapter Fourteen

THE HOAX

O **la:** The original plan was to make the "lynching" at 10:00 PM, but Jussie was in New York, and his flight was delayed. He sent Bola messages through Instagram to push the time back to midnight. Then one, then two. Jussie was finally on the plane, so the attack was on for 2:00 AM.

By this point, I'm ready to be done with this. We were waiting to leave to head to the scene, the stage, where we would perform our roles. Jussie wanted us to leave our phones at home. He was worried they would fall out during the 'attack.' Thinking back, I can't help wondering if he was worried they would ping off a nearby cell tower when the police began investigating. At the time, Jussie's concern was valid. I put on a watch. And waited and waited.

Finally, the time was set. Jussie should be in the area around 2 AM. We dressed in clothing that would keep us warm as well as hide our identities. The slit in our mask showed only our eyes.

I ordered an Uber that then took us to a predetermined location, where we got a taxi to take us to the scene. We stayed in character the entire time. If we spoke, we used the white southern voice. Bola and I decided to use the Southern voices. We wanted to make sure no one would think it was us.

While we waited for Jussie, we began rehearsing and going over our parts the same as we would do for any acting gig. My character's name was Bubba. Bola decided to give me a name for my character.

Bola: When we got to the place, we began to ask ourselves where to go after we had made the 'attack.' None of us had thought about that. We quickly surveyed the area. There was a river nearby, and we agreed to go that way. Out of the corner of my eye, I saw Jussie. We were a short distance from the spot where Jussie wanted us to do it. Chicago was in the middle of a polar vortex. It was -20 degrees! We had on three coats, three pairs of socks, three pairs of gloves, with hand warmers! Even with multiple layers, we were still freezing!

No one would be out wandering around at that temperature! Unless it was a job they were being paid for. I told myself that when this role was finished, I would be heading off to Nigeria, where it would be much warmer! This was one time I couldn't wait for that Nigerian heat! We hurried back just as Jussie was walking across the street. We made sure we walked the way an old white man would. The character was key. The lights were on, the camera set, and now for the action! "Empire faggot!"

As Jussie turned, I could see he was on the phone as he planned. I found out later it was with his music manager, Brandon Z. Moore.

Jussie asked me what I'd said.

In character, I said, "This is MAGA country!" I threw a fake punch and made it appear like we were tussling before throwing him to the ground. This wasn't a hard hit as I pulled my punch the way he wanted me to. It looked like I threw him to the ground. All of this had been choreographed beforehand. I gave him a fake kick. "Nigger, this is MAGA country!" Then I balled up my knuckle and gave him a nuggie on his face, so he would have a little bruise to add to the story.

I was trying to be inconspicuous but also make it look good for the camera. Jussie wanted everything to look real especially the punch. He wanted me to hold back on that, but to make it look like I wasn't. It was an Oscar-winning performance. It was very realistic. It appeared like I was hitting him over and over again in the face. I let him get in a few 'punches' so he could say he fought back.

Ola: From the moment we were picked up by the Uber, we were in full character. We wanted to be sure no one had any idea we were black men or local. Our identities had to come off as Southern white men. We practiced our southern accents and spoke in them when we spoke. We had every inch of us covered except our eyes. There was no way anyone would have thought we were black. It was freezing that night.

Bola and I played our roles perfectly; the cab driver and the Uber driver told the police we were white men. While Bola was tussling with Jussie on the ground, I began sprinkling bleach on top of his shirt. I was in the process of putting the noose around his neck when I saw lights coming our way. I had the noose about to loop it over his head, but the moment I saw the lights, I was done. I let it go and ran.

My first thought was, what have we gotten ourselves into? We made a point of never doing anything to attract police attention, and we did this! What were we thinking?

Looking back now, things could have gone wrong in so many ways. What if someone saw us and called the police? What if the person on the phone with Jussie hung up and called the police? At the time, nothing like that crossed my mind. Probably because we saw it as an acting gig; that's all it was to us. That and helping a friend.

Bola: I saw the lights. My first thought was, damn, someone is looking at us! Let's get out of here! Let's get out of this! I ran towards the river as we were supposed to. I knew Ola was running too. We passed by security that flashed a light in our faces as we were running away. We ran up some stairs, then down Columbus, then another flight of stairs. After a moment or two, we heard sirens getting closer. I was scared! I kept thinking, oh shit! What's going on? Sirens mean police! Were they coming towards us? How did someone know about this? I was so nervous.

Ola and I didn't stop running until we reached Sheraton Hotel, where we got a cab. We had the cab take us to Wrigley and drop us four blocks from our house. Then we walked the rest of the way.

It was between three and four in the morning when we got there. I went to sleep as I knew we were going to be up soon to travel to Nigeria.

Ola did the same. I could still feel the cold. It was in my bones. Nigeria would take care of that!

The next morning, while we were getting our stuff together to go to the airport, we heard about the attack. I had heard nothing from Jussie at this point.

Chapter Fifteen

WAIT...WHAT?

Bola: Upon waking, a friend of mine from high school sent me an article that TMZ had posted about Jussie being attacked. My first thought was Jussie's plan worked. That it had worked the way he wanted it to, it was a job well done! I had a plane to catch, so I began to get ready for that.

Ola: I saw the article Bola's friend sent. Like him, I thought, hey, it worked! Then I went back to getting ready to leave. I was excited to be going to Nigeria to see family as well as audition for *Big Brother Naija*. I wasn't thinking about the 'attack.' We had done what we were paid to do; that role was over. Time to move on to the next one.

Bola: We ended up on a flight that was practically empty. We were able to take an entire row each to ourselves. We sat near each other, but not in the same row. We had a layover in Turkey for twenty-one hours. We got a hotel room for the duration. This was mostly the way our flights were normally.

Jussie called me from a new number. I didn't ask why he was calling from a different number. Honestly, at this point, I thought the 'attack' had done what Jussie wanted it to, and I'd moved on to thinking about why we were going to Nigeria. He explained he had given my information to some people that they might call me. I was like, cool. It wasn't something that bothered me for any reason.

Thinking back on it, he must have done that because he knew the police were investigating already. At the time, it was the furthest thought from my mind.

Ola: Knowing the facts now, we see he told the police the same night. Not once did we think he would do such a thing when he asked us to make the fake 'attack.'

I found out later when Jussie was on *Good Morning America,* his manager Frank called the police after Jussie returned to his apartment.

Bola: Turns out the manager Jussie was talking to wasn't the one that called the police. It was the one he'd left at his apartment when he went out to get a sub at 2:00 in the morning in the middle of a Polar vortex!

They said hindsight is 20/20. Looking back, there are so many things I should have questioned, but at the time, it was an acting gig, and Jussie was the star. At one point, I saw where he was being interviewed, and he was asked why he didn't call the police immediately. Jussie said he was a black gay man in America. It was like he was trying to come up with excuses as to why he didn't, and he had the perfect reason for not calling.

Since the 'attack,' people have pointed out that we just happened to leave town right after 'attacking' Jussie. Sort of like it was an escape so the police wouldn't arrest us. That isn't true. Ola and I purchased our tickets in October. This trip had been planned for months. We were going to Nigeria to audition for *Big Brother Naija.* It is a very popular show, much like *Big Brother* in America.

Ola: My mother and father had returned to Nigeria a while before. They went every so often, staying for months at a time, sometimes years. Our father and mother and a couple of family friends picked us up the way they normally did. This was just a normal visit home except for the audition. Nothing we haven't done before.

Bola: We landed at Murtala Mohammed Airport, MMA, in Lagos. Our parents and other family members were there to greet us like always. For a day or so, we spent time with family catching up. The audition was on February 2, 2019. We were in different lines for hours. There were thousands of people there! It's a very popular show in Nigeria.

After what felt like an eternity, we were finally inside to sit down. We were ready for this. Then, we were informed the only way to be on the show was if we had a Nigerian passport. That was disappointing!

We told them we could get one, but they wouldn't hear of it. We left there feeling horrible! We had been so set on getting on this show. We had no doubt they would have liked us and our character if we had just been given a chance. Reluctantly we went home. We waited all those hours to be sent away without even auditioning!

Ola: It was disappointing not to have a chance to even audition, but it was a fun experience. We knew to find out those kinds of things first before going forward. With each knockdown, we get right back up again.

Bola: We weren't scheduled to fly back to America until February twelfth. While we were in Nigeria, we visited my grandfather on my father's side. At that time, he was 89 or 90. We always made time to visit him. He is the one that knows all of our family history and explains it to us. That time with him will always be treasured.

Ola: At this point, we don't know that the police were involved. We were doing things we would normally do while in Nigeria.

Bola: When in Nigeria, we go to a lot of parties. Big extravagant loud, and fun parties. There is a lot of food, dancing, and spraying of money. That's when they just quickly shuffle money out of their hands, bill after bill, towards the other person.

Ola: Between seeing our family and the parties, we didn't really have any time to be watching TV to see what was going on with Jussie in America. Our trip was coming to an end, and it's time for us to get ready to head back to America. I was on Twitter and saw from the Chicago Police Department's Twitter account that police were investigating the 'attack' on Jussie. This was the first time we knew of the police's involvement. Bola began to check it every day after that leading up to when we were going back to the States. Celebrities were posting in support of Jussie. Everyone was talking about it!

Bola: There was a post from Anthony Guglielmi, the spokesman for the Chicago Police Department, talking about looking at videos and asking for witnesses. There was nothing at this point that they could give out to the public as a description of who to look for. Right away, I had a bad feeling; they already knew that it was us. They didn't offer any information other than that, but intuitively, I felt they would be waiting for us upon our return to Chicago. Ola showed the post to my brother and shared the feeling of unease I had.

Ola: He did, but I thought he was crazy.

Bola: It wasn't just that image that had me thinking something wasn't right. It was something else I had done for Jussie. He hit me up on January 24th to ask me for a meal and workout plan. It hit me suddenly that this could be something he had asked for as a way to corroborate on his story about an attack. But at the same time, I couldn't believe my friend would have done such a thing.

Looking back on it now, I know that was his original intent. He knew that upon reporting the 'attack' to the police, they would be investigating all of his acquaintances, and the check he used to pay us, would be questioned, especially if we became a suspects. He couldn't risk that check appearing to be what it really was, payment for the 'attack.' That is why he put in the memo line on the check that it was for a meal plan and workout program.

I don't know why Jussie thought anyone would believe that check was for a meal plan and an exercise plan. At that time, we only charged

$50-$80 for meal plans and $30-$50 for exercise plans; if we charged that, we would never have any business! Not to mention we were friends! I would have given him a friend and family discount!

Ola: We didn't mention anything about the 'attack' to our family, not that we were involved or that it had happened. I'm sure they may have heard about it at some point, but if so, nothing was said to us. As far as I was concerned, this had been an acting gig, and that was it.

Bola: An acting gig and helping out a friend. I had no idea Jussie was going to go to the police. Not once had he implied something like that would happen. It was supposed to be a quick little incident that he could have released on social media to show he was in 'danger' like the note he received showed and that he wasn't able to take care of himself, I think. I don't know for sure, as he never said.

There were a number of celebrities who sent their support through social media to Jussie when word got out about the hoax.

Actress Viola Davis tweeted:

> "OMG!! THIS is why the LGBTQ community continue to fight to be seen and PROTECTED against hate! We ALL have to take this racist and homophobic act of violence very personally! My arms are around you @jussesmollett. You are loved!"

Lee Daniels, director of Empire, tweeted:

> "We are all better than that. America is better than that… And no racist f**k can come in and do the things that they did to you. Hold your head up, Jussie. I'm with you."

Multi-talented John Legend's tweet in support of Jussie reads:

> "Sending love to Jussie and the Smollett family after this horrific attack. We support you and pray that you find peace and justice."

Actress Vivica A Fox played Jussie's aunt on Empire. She tweeted:

> "I'm just now hearing the news about the senseless hate attack on my #EMPIRE Nephew @jussiesmollett. I'M SO ANGRY AND HURT ABOUT THIS! SPREAD LOVE NOT HATE! PRAYERS UP TO U NEPHEW!"

This is the tweet Ola and Bola saw while they were in Nigeria.

Anthony Gugliemi tweeted:

> "Statement on #ChicagoPolice hate crime investigation. We are taking these allegations very seriously and encourage anyone with information to report anonymously to cpdtip. com"

In response to this tweet from the Office of the Superintendent Communication and New Affairs.

> "Overnight, the Chicago Police Department received a report of a possible racially-charged assault and battery involving a cast member of the television show Empire. Given the severity of the allegations, we are taking this investigation very seriously and treating it as a possible hate crime. Detectives are currently working to gather video, identify potential witnesses and establish an investigative timeline. The victim is fully cooperating with investigators and we ask anyone with information about this incident to contact Area Central Detectives. At 312-747-8382 or anonymously to www.cpdtip.com"

A short time later, Anthony Giuliani tweeted this:

> "UPDATE: We continue to seek any available evidence/video to identify possible offenders in this case. Anyone who may hv been in the area of 300 E North Water St. btwn 1-3a should send info to www.cpdtip.com. Thus far we have not found anything to be able to put out a description."

Chapter Sixteen

YOU HAVE THE RIGHT TO
REMAIN SILENT

Ola: As we were getting on the plane on February 13, 2019, Bola told me he had an uneasy feeling about what we would find upon arriving in Chicago. He shared his same concerns with me, but we still got on the plane.

Bola: I had a painting from a Nigerian artist as well as my luggage. We had a layover in Turkey again. Upon getting on the plane from Turkey to Chicago, we didn't see each other. We weren't sitting together on the plane. I am not even sure where his seat was.

Ola: That feeling I'd had in Nigeria kept hitting me as we got closer to Chicago. It was a feeling of dread. A dread of what we were walking into. At the same time, I was thinking to myself; I haven't done anything wrong, so why was I feeling this way?

Bola: I didn't know it, but Ola and I were having similar feelings and questioning why we felt this way. I heard from Jussie once while in Nigeria. He texted about his exercise program. That was the only time. I kept asking myself why I was feeling this way. I hadn't done anything. Why was I worried? My brother and I had helped a man I considered a friend, a brother. Jussie had given us a script, and we had followed it. Why was I worried? Because the police were involved, and there was no reason for them to be! My subconscious pointed this out. I wasn't seated near Ola, so I couldn't share my concerns with him.

Ola: I had a feeling the second we touched down that something was going to happen once I was off the plane. What, I didn't know. The feeling wouldn't pass. I couldn't talk it over with my brother. I don't know exactly what I was expecting, but I wasn't expecting to be arrested. I hadn't done anything wrong. Police were involved. There was not supposed to be any police. We hadn't really attacked Jussie. It was a skit made up by Jussie that he paid us to do. Nothing Bola and I had done was illegal. I had nothing to be worried about.

As I got in line to go through customs, I knew I had been right to feel like something was up. Airline security was picking people out to have their baggage searched. But it wasn't the random way they normally did it. They were checking passports. They knew our names and had a copy of our picture! I knew then that they were looking for me and my brother!

There was nothing I could do except follow them to get my luggage and then to the room they indicated. As I walked through the door to that room, I glanced around to see if my brother had been detained too.

Bola: Upon getting on the plane, Ola and I were separated. I couldn't see him from where I was sitting while on the plane or when I was getting off. I think he got off before me. Seeing custom agents checking passports, I remembered the feeling I had in Nigeria and the feeling Ola had mentioned he had as well. Now I knew why. I glanced around, trying to find my brother in the crowd.

I wasn't surprised when the agent I gave my passport to said to follow him. We retrieved my baggage and the painting I'd brought from Nigeria before he led me into a room. I once more looked for Ola before going inside that room. As my bags were searched thoroughly, I reminded myself I had done nothing illegal; therefore, I had no reason to be nervous.

Checking my bags would reveal nothing illegal was in them. A few moments and, I would be able to walk out that door with my bags and meet my brother out front.

Just because the police were involved in what was supposed to be a social media incident had nothing to do with me. They didn't know who I was. The social media we had seen earlier showed that the police were actively searching for the two black figures seen in a video from the time of the incident, two white men. The police were releasing no more information on it. There was a part of me that said the police knew it was my brother and I and were waiting to arrest us.

This feeling stayed with me the entire flight, but I kept telling myself Ola, and I had not done anything illegal. We helped our friend with a problem he wanted help with, and nothing we did was against the law! At the same time, innocent people have been accused before. I think that was what led to my uneasy feeling. A part of me thought I was being paranoid, but low and behold, I wasn't!

Looking back, I think the police were already doubting what Jussie said was true. I don't know why they would have at that point, but something about the way they handled us made me feel like they had doubts.

Ola: Upon the completion of my baggage search, the customs officer sent me on my way. The moment I went through those doors, I began looking for my brother. Had he been detained as well? Hopefully, he was waiting outside. Not more than a few steps from that room and I had detectives blocking my exit.

The detectives showed me their badges and asked me to come with them. I was asked to hand over my phone. At the time, I had three phones with me. I had taken it to Nigeria for my mom, but it wouldn't work there, so she sent it back with me. The other two were mine. When I handed them over, I was told to open them as I had them locked.

I have heard in the past that Chicago Police have been known to rough up a suspect, but they were very nice to me. I was told my rights and handcuffed. This wasn't my first time in handcuffs since I was taken in for riding my bike on the sidewalk. They tried to ask me a few questions, but when they refused to tell me why I was being arrested, I asked for a lawyer. Until I had an idea of what I was being accused of, I wasn't saying another word.

My first thought was, my girl, is going to kill me! I had been in Nigeria for two weeks, and Valentine's Day was the next day. She was not going to be happy I was arrested. I thought I needed this situation to end quickly so I could see my girl and get some flowers and some candy for her!

Looking back, that was an odd thing for me to be thinking about, but at the same time, it was the only thought because I knew I had not done anything wrong. This little detainment would end with me walking out the door. The question was would it be in time to get my girl something special for Valentine's Day? Not once did I think I was going to prison for 'lynching' Jussie. The 'attack' was fake, a hoax. I just needed the police to see that. Just because Jussie was a celebrity, I trusted that the truth would be revealed and I would be sent home by day's end.

Not once when we talked about the 'attack,' practiced it, or actually did it, did I think Jussie would go to the police. If I had, I would never have expected him to pretend the 'attack' was real! I didn't know him as well as my brother, but my brother trusted him; therefore, I had no reason to doubt him. Looking back, I am dumbfounded that he lied and stuck to the lie the entire time, even to this day!

By this point, I still had no idea where my brother was.

Bola: When I walked out of that room with my bags and painting, I once more searched for my brother. I hoped he was outside somewhere. A moment later, I was met by a few detectives who were really nice. They were friendly and said they'd like to talk to me.

They took me into a room. I wasn't told why I was being detained. I asked for a lawyer. An hour and a half later, they escorted me outside. They didn't cuff me until then. The moment we were out of the airport, their nice friendly manner disappeared. They read me my rights but still didn't tell me what I was being charged with. They were asking questions and asking whether I wanted to talk, but when I'd ask what they were there for, they wouldn't say. If they couldn't answer my questions, I wouldn't answer theirs.

As they were preparing to put me in the police car, they asked for my phone. Once I handed it over, they asked for me to unlock it. I refused. Why should I open my phone for them? People have asked me why I refused if I had nothing to hide. The answer is simple. If they couldn't tell me why I was being arrested, I could be stubborn and keep my phone locked. I used that magic word you were supposed to use when the cops handcuffed you. Lawyer.

I had never had handcuffs on before…at least not police handcuffs.

I had texts from Jussie on my phone where he had asked me to get him some weed and molly. All of our conversations were on there. No way was I handing over my phone until I knew exactly why I was being arrested. Until I had a lawyer, I wasn't offering to do anything! I knew there were times the police got a little…confused, I'll say.

As that police car pulled away from Chicago O'Hare Airport, I wondered where my brother was.

Being arrested at the airport.

Bola with the painting he brought back from Nigeria.

The painting has yet to be returned to Bola from the FBI.

Chapter Seventeen

CALL MY LAWYER

Ola: I was taken to the local precinct. I had no knowledge if Bola was detained or arrested. Had he gotten through customs and was wondering where I was? The one thing I knew for sure was that if my brother hadn't been detained, he would be trying to find me. Before I was put in a cell by myself, I was fingerprinted and had my mugshot taken.

As I was placed in that holding cell, my thoughts were of my girl and my brother. Time seemed to stand still in that cell. I didn't know what time it was or the day. I knew I needed an attorney, but I had no idea who to call. I didn't eat or drink while I was there. It was offered, but I wouldn't take it. I don't know what I was thinking by declining all food and drinks offered. At the time, I was being stubborn.

Periodically, I would be taken from the cell and asked if I was ready to talk. When I wouldn't say anything, I'd be sent back to stare at the walls until the next time they wanted to give it a go.

Sitting in that cell was excruciating. The longer I was there, the longer it seemed. I lost all track of the time. I had no idea if it was daylight or night. I have heard of people not able to handle the emptiness committing suicide. I never had that thought, but I can see why some people would.

One of the worst feelings I had was when I was sitting in the cell, not knowing exactly what was going on or what time of day it was. The not knowing, not having any sense of time at all, just sitting in that cell. The silence that surrounded me could easily drive you crazy. Nothing to read, nothing to do but stare at the walls while your mind runs through every possible scenario. That was the worst thing about being there. The silence. It was deafening.

Bola: I was taken to the main precinct, 51. At the time, I had no idea where that was. I was fingerprinted and had a mugshot made before they put me in a holding cell. They asked me if I was ready to talk. I said no, I wanted my lawyer. They asked me who my lawyer was, and I told them the only lawyer I knew, Abdallah Law. There was always this ad on the radio about this lawyer, and when I needed one, it was the only one I could think of. They were supposed to call my lawyer for me, but they never did. I don't know if the man was even a criminal attorney!

I felt isolated. There were no other inmates around me. Sitting there in that cell minute after minute, hour after hour, day after day, I had one thought running through my mind. Where was my brother? If he was arrested, is he in a cell somewhere under the same roof I was in? Had he been taken to another precinct? By this time, I had a pretty good idea this had something to do with Jussie. I was almost certain Ola had been arrested too. Why remained to be seen?

I was offered food and drink but declined it. I didn't have an appetite. I felt like I was in a cage at the zoo, only there were no people walking by looking at me other than the occasional cop asking if I was ready to talk. I paced back and forth behind those bars feeling more and more like a caged lion. I had no sense of time, no sense of what was going on.

Was anyone looking for me? Had anyone realized I had virtually vanished? It began to mess with my psyche a little. I can see why people in solitary confinement would go crazy. After those few days in that cell, I know one thing for certain humans shouldn't be locked up! I would never do anything that would result in that again! I may have had a moment or two where I could understand people who couldn't take it and just ended it all. But I never thought of doing so!

Occasionally I was removed from the cell and taken to a room that just had a bench. It was for questioning, but I wouldn't talk. Then I would be returned to my cell. I would have preferred to stay in that room as opposed to returning to the cell. It was disgusting! The toilet smelled horrible! If I had to shit, there was no way I was going to do it in that! Looking back, I should have shit on the floor and left it for them to clean up!

In a way, I guess I was better off than my brother in that cell. The officer attendant downstairs, I knew from acting. He let me use his phone. I called my oldest brother or one of my sisters. The guy, David, kept asking me what I was doing there. What had I done? I wouldn't say, as I didn't know exactly why I was there. I know that some people will start talking and reasoning why they did or didn't do something in the hopes the police will let them go. The one thing I was certain of was no matter who it was; I needed to keep my mouth shut! In that, I was certain!

I'd seen movies and TV shows that show how to behave when arrested. I never thought that one day I would have to use that knowledge myself. No lawyer, not talking! They had yet to call the lawyer I asked for, which was wrong of them! I don't know the people at Abadulla Law Firm. If they had called them, I don't know how I would have paid for them. They still should have called! Although, I didn't do anything to need a lawyer.

Ola: When I was given a phone call, I called my girlfriend. Not an attorney, my girlfriend. People ask why I didn't call a lawyer; I tell them I had no reason to call a lawyer. I hadn't broken any laws. That's how worried I was about possible charges. I knew I hadn't done anything to be arrested for. My concern was keeping my girlfriend from wanting to murder me for screwing up Valentine's Day!

I hadn't even gotten flowers or anything. I had planned to do that after I got back from Nigeria. I had planned to do Valentine's Day up good! A Valentine's she would never forget. I guess she remembers that Valentine's Day, though not why I had planned. The good thing was she didn't break up with me! That relationship ended much later.

Bola: The way we got a lawyer is interesting! My mother was an Uber driver. A while back, I'm talking a year or so, she gave a lawyer a ride. The lawyer gave my mother her card in case she was ever in need of a lawyer. I called my oldest brother, who was at our house. He called my mother, who remembered that lawyer's card. She had to find it, but once she did, she called the number on the card. No one answered. It was in the middle of the night. Gloria, Gloria Schmidt Rodriquez, told me after she became our lawyer, she hadn't recognized the number. It was a number from Nigeria, after all. She called back once she heard the message.

I had no idea of any of this. I used my only phone call to my brother. I didn't know if he was looking for a lawyer or if he'd told my parents. I couldn't tell you how long I'd been in that cell, before that phone call or after.

Ola: At this point, I had no idea if I had a lawyer or anyone else coming. Once I said I wanted a lawyer, the detectives knew I wasn't going to answer any questions. I had no idea my mother had driven Gloria somewhere and now had her card. I didn't speak to them until Gloria arrived. Not one time was Jussie's name mentioned to me until Gloria arrived.

After what seemed like forever, an officer came to my cell and told me my lawyer had arrived. Lawyer? Who had called me a lawyer? My girlfriend? No reason for her to do so. Had she called my parents and told them I was being held? Had they hired a lawyer?

I was taken to that room with the bench, only this time, it wasn't empty. I don't know what I expected from my attorney, but it wasn't what I got. Gloria was this little spitfire. Right off, she tells me she is my lawyer, whom my mother had hired.

She told me I needed to eat, indicating some food the police had supplied. I refused. I refused the food and talked to her. I had to be sure before I would tell her anything.

Bola: When I was told my lawyer showed up, for a moment, I thought maybe they had called the guy from the radio. But that was a fleeting thought. I seriously doubted that guy would be my attorney. I'm not sure he would be a good fit for my case if I had a case.

By this time, I am tired and hungry and ready to be done with this.

I was taken to the room with the bench to meet my lawyer. I had been in that jail for hours. All that time with no food or drink. With no one to talk to. I spent hours wondering where my brother was.

I hoped whoever my lawyer was, they would be able to answer that question. I took one look at Gloria and was like no way; she is my lawyer! I was sure the police were playing games on me. I mean, they can be tricky! Was this a ploy to get me to talk? I was very skeptical. I was a little apprehensive of Gloria initially.

She explained how she came to be my attorney. It sounded comical in a way. What were the odds my mother would give a lawyer a lift and keep her card? One in a million? Nothing against Gloria, but I didn't know her, and her story sounded crazy! She tried to get me to eat, but I wouldn't.

She left me in the room and went to speak to the officers.

Ola: When Gloria returned with her assistant, she had a vegetable tray. She told me to eat it, but I once more refused. It was the weirdest thing; she and her assistant began eating them and even putting some in her bag and pockets.

Gloria convinced me she was there to help me and Bola. She told me Bola was there in the same precinct as me. Finally, I knew where my brother was! Gloria convinced me she truly was there to help me and Bola.

I told Gloria everything from how I knew Jussie to the fake "attack." She informed me Bola and I were suspects in the "attack."

Gloria told me Bola refused to talk or eat. I convinced her that I would be able to convince him to talk if they would let me see him.

Bola: Gloria joined me in the room with the bench once again. This time she had my brother with her. I hugged him, thankful to finally know where he was.

Gloria informed us we were considered suspects. I told her what happened.

After hearing the same thing from us, she convinced us to talk to the detectives. I had yet to open my phone for them. Gloria informed me they had a warrant to do so.

Gloria explained how the "attack" was all over the media. A video of two men running away from the scene was BIG news. BIG NEWS! Not just in America. Globally. Every member of my family, be they in America or Nigeria, knew about the "attack."

Suddenly this acting gig was labeled as an attack. Not just an attack, a hate crime. Jussie had gone to the police reporting that two white southern men attacked him and put a noose around his neck, and dumped bleach on him. All while saying racial and homophobic slurs.

I was dumbfounded! How had helping a friend turned into a media circus? There wasn't any video of the "attack" What happened to the video from the camera Jussie had pointed out?

Gloria assured us it was safe to talk to the detectives without an immunity deal. As no crime had been committed, we had no need for immunity. She wanted us to talk to the detectives. We were not criminals.

With Gloria at my side, I told them everything. I explained how Jussie approached me with the letter. They went through my phone, matching texts to what I was saying.

After forty-seven hours of a forty-eight-hour hold, I finally told them everything.

Gloria was able to be our attorney without it being an issue. If we had to have separate lawyers, as sometimes codefendants are required, I don't know what would have happened.

We don't like any dealings with the police that is a normal feeling in our culture. Not to mention the days of solitude I'd had in a cell had me a little nervous. That, combined with the texts on my phone about getting Jussie narcotics, had me a little worried.

Gloria informed me there was no need to be.

The police were already suspicious of the story Jussie told. They just needed us to fill in what they didn't know.

I knew Ola, and I hadn't done anything wrong, but when you are a black man in America and some other countries, you learn to be cautious when it comes to the police. Chicago, unfortunately, has a bad reputation for how they handle some of their detainees. What we did wasn't criminally wrong. It may have been seen by some as morally wrong, but to me, I was helping out a friend doing a short film.

Ola: I knew we hadn't done anything illegal. The detectives were just doing their due diligence. I don't know if we had spoken to the police prior to Gloria coming if we would have been released. There's no way to know for sure that they knew we were not involved in an actual attack.

Honestly, I would have been skeptical if the police had approached me saying something like that without Gloria present. Looking back on it, I would not change how I did when the police arrested me. I would have kept my mouth shut until I knew for certain they were not going to hold me accountable for an attack that was not even real.

Once the police said we were free to go, I was ready to run for the door. At the time, I had no idea what would be waiting for me there. Gloria was just filling us in on how massive this incident had become to the world.

Bola: Once we told the entire story, one of the officers called the "attack" a hoax. I hadn't thought of it like that before. What I saw as an acting gig, the world saw as a hate crime, and the detectives saw it as a hoax.

The police told me the words I had been longing to hear. You are free to go. I wanted to run for the door.

In a surprise twist, the detectives had us go out the back door to avoid the horde of media waiting to pounce at the front of the station. They were concerned about how many microphones would be shoved in our faces when they got their first look at the 'attackers.' In a way going out the back was like we escaped.

After days without food, we needed substance. Gloria and the detectives took us to Uptown BBQ. That was the best BBQ I ever had.

Bola: While we were staring at those cell bars, the police executed a search warrant on our house. My oldest brother was there, but they busted the door anyway. They left the door hanging open. We found out later they had found multiple guns and ammo. Some media outlets said cocaine had been found, but that wasn't true. There were more media in front of our house. I don't believe anyone had been inside the house.

The police had us get some things before they took us to a local hotel. They were putting us up until we testified before the grand jury.

Chapter Eighteen

IS IT REALLY FREEDOM IF I'M STILL LOCKED UP?

Bola: The police detective dropped us at the hotel with instructions to stay put. A few officers were assigned to keep the media out and us in.

Ola: We left one jail for another. Just because this one was nicer didn't make it anything but a cell. We were on lockdown until we could testify before the grand jury whenever that happened.

Bola: At least we were able to see each other in the new cell. The officers weren't that bad. It was just the lack of freedom that bothered me.

A couple of times, they would let us go out and grab a burger incognito, of course. Don't worry; it wasn't as Southern white men!

Ola: Anytime we left our room, at least three officers accompanied us. Even to work out in the gym. If we had any visitors come to see us be it my girlfriend, brother, or his wife, anyone had to be approved. There was no chance anyone would slip by them even if they tried. I thought that was a bit much. There was no way Jussie would try to shut us up. He wasn't that kind of man.

Bola: I wouldn't have thought he would tell the police we attacked him, but he did.

Ola: True. I think it had more to do with keeping the media away. Gloria had insisted that we not speak to the media. I had no idea how a grand jury worked. How long would it take to get a jury? Once that was done, how long before we testified?

Gloria explained how a grand jury worked. She said it wasn't as formal as a normal courtroom. There wouldn't be a judge or lawyer save for the prosecutor. The prosecutor would instruct those chosen for the jury to listen to the testimonies of my brother and me and anyone else who testified.

Bola: All the texts and Instagram messages between Jussie and me would be shown to the jurors. Once the evidence and testimonies were done, the grand jury would make the decision to indict or not.

Ola: I was ready. The sooner Bola and I testified, the sooner we could get on with our lives! Finally, the day came. I was ready to tell those good people chosen to decide Jussie's fate the truth. I wanted them to see what happened when helping a friend. Our lives were turned upside down because we helped a brother out.

Finally, the day arrived! I was ready to tell exactly what happened. And then it was postponed! Then the next day, Jussie's lawyer had some excuse, and once again, it was postponed! What the hell was the problem? Were they trying to find a way to get Jussie off before we even had a chance to testify? Were they that worried about what Bola and I would say? Or was it they knew what we would say was true because their client had told them so, and they were hoping to delay the indictment they knew would come? Whatever the reason, I was annoyed as hell. We needed to do this. I had a life to get back to!

Finally, the day arrived! I didn't get excited as we had been down this road twice before. If this was canceled again, I was going to go crazy! Life in a hotel is not as fun as you might think it would be! At this point, I still didn't know exactly what the charges against Jussie were.

I took the stand and told everyone in that courtroom exactly what went down leading up to that night. I answered every question thrown at me truthfully and precisely. I didn't add anything to my answers to make them sound more eloquent. There was no need. The truth was on my side.

I held nothing back. This was my chance to get the truth out there, so the lies circulating around were shown as what they were. Lies! Why had I used bleach if Jussie had said gasoline? Bleach made more sense as it would be something I would have on hand as opposed to gas. Jussie also didn't want to have any video of me getting the gas.

The noose was what I think sealed it as me telling the truth. I had no idea how to tie a noose. Bola didn't either. I had to look it up! Talking to those people, the jury, I realized how messed up it was for Jussie to ask us to put a noose around his neck!

If you look back through history, you find more than one black person, regardless of where they live, was hanged! History was littered with images of black men, and women strung up in a tree! This is something Jussie would know. I think he wanted the noose because of that! He knew how such a symbol would fuel the mass outcry!

Looking back, I didn't think anything about that. I should have, but as I said, these were props for the scene. When I saw that light coming that night, I was in the middle of putting the noose on him. I dropped it and ran. When I left Jussie that night, the noose was on his face.

When all the craziness was over, I saw a cop's bodycam footage of Jussie wearing the noose! Which meant he had to put that noose on himself! The really twisted thing about this was not just that Jussie put the noose on himself; it was that he wore it until the police showed up!

Roughly an hour after the alleged attack! His manager was there in his apartment with him. He was the one who called the police. How did Jussie explain why he wouldn't take off the noose?

It astounds me that he would do that! Was he really oblivious to how twisted that was? The officer asked him if he wanted to remove it! Why would you need to be asked to remove a noose? Not only a cop but a white cop! How could Jussie miss how ludacris this was! He gave the cop some sort of excuse about wearing it until they could see it. But for an hour!

Bola: Ola and I talked about that recently. Like Ola, I didn't think anything of it at the time. On behalf of my brother and I, we want to apologize for the noose. We weren't the ones who chose to include such a thing, but we did. We are so sorry for any hurt we caused anyone.

Ola: Jussie owes everyone an apology, including us!

My testimony took a while, but I didn't want to leave anything out. I was direct and clear in my answers. I wanted that jury to have all the facts they needed to make the right decision.

Bola: I was precise in the details, going through the texts and explaining what was going on with each one.

The day seemed extra long, but I didn't mind. I wanted to get this over with so we could get our lives back. Before this, Ola and I were going to different auditions. Acting paid some of the bills but not all. Ola and I were bouncers at a place called Whiskey Business and another place called Granero. Life in a hotel waiting for the grand jury to convene had taken that away.

We could barely go anywhere without someone in the media or TMZ following us. TMZ seemed to be almost stalking us. They seemed to be there no matter where we were, except inside the hotel or the courtroom. As an actor, TMZ would feature you on their show, which would be great if it was for something other than this! TMZ was one of the first to report the 'attack.' They were one of the first to report we'd been detained, as well as the attack being a hoax. They might have been the first ones to use the word hoax.

At some point, someone within the media began to call me Abel. I have never gone by Abel. I have the Team Abel Instagram, but I do not use Abel as my name. I go by Bola. For some reason, one person used Abel, and then everyone did! That right there told me how good the media would be at reporting the truth!

They couldn't even get my name right! Seriously, how hard is it to get my name right? Bola is a far cry from Abel! My name is Abimbola. Where do you see Abel in that? Nowhere! Bola is there, though, at the end.

Yet there it was again and again in news articles. 'Abel Osundairo testifies before the grand jury.' 'Abel Osundairo was friends with Jussie.' It went on and on! If you look me up on the internet right now with Bola Osundairo, it will pull up Abel Osundairo.

Anytime the media saw me, I heard, 'Abel, why did you attack Jussie?'

'Abel, were you in a relationship with Jussie?'

'Abel, are you a lover scorned?'

'Abel! Abel! Abel!' The name was just one issue I had. Everywhere we went, cameras and microphones were put in our faces.

Everyone had questions! Questions we weren't allowed to answer.

'Abel, did you attack Jussie because he broke up with you?'

'Abel, why did you agree to attack Jussie?'

'Abel, are you gay?'

'Ola, are you homophobic?'

'Ola, did you attack Jussie because you hate gay people?'

The questions were bad enough, but the claims being printed and talked about on every outlet were much worse. 'Abel was Jussie's drug dealer!'

'Abel spent time with Jussie in a bathhouse.'

'Nigerian brothers attacked Jussie in an attempt to be hired as his security!'

Abel is forced by their homophobic brother to attack Jussie to prove he's not gay.'

'Nigerian brothers attempted to blackmail Jussie asking for one million each to keep quiet.'

'Abel masturbated with Jussie in the bathhouse.'

Ola: Suddenly, my brother and I were known as the Nigerian Brothers, which is fine. It was like how the media had screwed up with Bola calling him Abel. A lot of the media thought we were born in Nigeria. This was more proof the media couldn't be trusted to report the truth.

The accusations got worse daily, and we couldn't dispute them! Gloria insisted we not talk to anyone! Family members were asking if some of the lies were true because we hadn't refuted them! That hurt! They knew me. They knew I wouldn't do any of what I was being accused of any more than they believed Bola would. They didn't understand why we weren't setting the record straight!

We had a drastic increase in inquiries in our business. But it was only inquiries. Maybe one out of fifty was actually interested in having us assist them with fitness and meal plans. The others were just trying to find out anything they could about the hoax; in the end, that was a waste of time for them. We didn't give out any information to those we worked with. This was our business. There was no way we were going to mix the two.

The only thing that was legit was the number of new followers we had on social media. I'm sure most of them were trolls hoping to find something they could blow out of proportion and use to go viral. What no one seemed to grasp then or now is that this wasn't what Jussie was portraying. This was a friend helping a friend while doing an acting gig.

Bola: The media was having fun making up nonsense for their magazines and shows. And we weren't allowed to do anything about it. I had to see articles and shows talking about how Jussie and I were in a relationship, and that was the reason he asked me to be his character stand-in. I wasn't able to contradict their lies as we were on a media lockdown.

Nigeria has made its thoughts on homosexuals known. Had anyone believed these lies, I could have died upon returning to Nigeria! That thought didn't cross my mind other than the fact I couldn't refute the lie!

We were told to lay low. How do you lay low when your face is on every paper and television screen? Suddenly, everyone wants to interview you for the position they are hiring for, but the only reason they do is to see what information you will share.

Once we testified, those cops that had kept an eye on us vanished, as did the police footing the bill. Gloria kept us there a couple more nights before we were able to go home. Someone had repaired the door. It was time for us to repair our lives and move on.

One of the first things we did was go out to grab a bite with friends. We were catching up and having a good time, finally free to go about our lives with no police, and we saw these people at another table with their phones pointed toward us with a microphone trying to hear what we were talking about. They would probably have sold it to TMZ or some magazine! I felt like I was in a fishbowl, and everyone was watching me while trying to coax me into the net. More than once, I asked myself why the hell I got myself into this mess!

Right before I went to Nigeria, I was signed to the biggest and the best talent agency in Chicago, Gray's Talent. They couldn't drop me fast enough after the incident! Their reasoning was they didn't think the relationship would be beneficial for either of us. It was a devastating blow to my goals. It was very difficult to get signed with them. They are the agency Hollywood turns to for actors! It felt like my life was crashing right before my eyes.

To this day, Jussie hasn't said anything about the attack being fake! Nor has he come out and said we were doing what he asked, what he paid us to do! How do you keep a lie going when you know the world knows the truth? It's almost like he has said it so many times that he believes the lie!

Keeping the bills paid required what few savings Ola and I had, as well as help from our parents. A few people I knew suggested going off to Nigeria and riding out the storm, then coming back and trying again. That would be like running away from problems, and I don't run away; I fight! I'm not saying that Nigeria is terrible, but what would going there accomplish?

Hiding was never an option! The only reason we'd been staying out of the public eye was because we were on lockdown by the police and Gloria. We wanted our freedom and our lives back. That freedom meant being free to defend ourselves too!

One media outlet actually stated if I had actually attacked Jussie, I would have left more than a simple scratch. My boxing abilities showed my skills. But did anyone report that over and over in the media? No, because something like that doesn't fit their narrative.

Every day there were more crazy stories coming out about us. In the media, everything we did was scrutinized. Our lack of rebuttal made the media worse. People were saying if it wasn't true, why didn't we say it? More than once, I had to bite my tongue to keep from setting some people straight! I had to bite my tongue so many times I'm surprised it's still there.

Ola: One story came out saying I was homophobic. That I just gave off a homophobic vibe. This guy was an extra on Empire who happened to be gay. He said he didn't feel comfortable around me because he could feel I didn't like gay people. One person said they overheard me on set one day say I couldn't be friends with a faggot, their word, not mine. I supposedly talked down to them and was hateful to them.

I have no idea who this guy was. There were numerous extras in almost every scene. They changed almost daily! This guy was after his fifteen minutes of fame. He knew the media was interested in any and all they could get, even if it wasn't true! And since we couldn't defend ourselves, it was considered true.

My character began as Chris Rock's character's bodyguard. Over the course of the show, my character ended up in prison. I'm in a cameo or two with some of the big names on the show.

In one scene, I am in the prison yard. This is where the photo of me and Lee Danials was taken. Supposedly, during this prison scene, I was saying derogatory remarks and homophobic slurs in between takes, I guess. I don't think the lie...claim had a lot of details. And that Bola was there and heard them! Bola and I never worked on *Empire* at the same time! This lie was told by two people! So, the media took it upon themselves to say it was true. Two people said it, after all! And I couldn't tell the media it was all lies!

While people were telling lies about my brother and Jussie being in a gay relationship, I was being accused of being homophobic! Not once did anyone stop and ask how I could be so close with my brother if he were gay, and I had an issue with gays! Not once! Anyone with common sense would have realized that was a lie! Everyone who knew us knew we were close brothers. Yet the media told their lies, and I could say nothing to quell them!

I was flabbergasted about how quickly people would believe a lie! No one was supporting me. Bola and my family weren't allowed to defend us. They were defaming my character, and I wasn't allowed to defend myself.

I asked Gloria if I was allowed to sue them. This particular person was in North Carolina, and it was something about jurisdiction, which basically meant I couldn't do a damn thing about the lies! It astounded me how people who knew nothing about me backed Jussie's story. He was a celebrity, and I guess they thought that meant he wouldn't lie! I wasn't a celebrity of his stature, so I must have made it all up!

Bola: On a post *The Daily Mail* posted on *Facebook* on February 28, 2019, that read 'Nigerian Brother in Jussie Smollett Case Made Anti-Gay Slurs on Set,' people commented horrible things! There's one post from a person I don't know that says:

> *"These extras aren't lying on these dudes. Y'all just never felt*
> *hollow, weird ass vibes, so y'all wouldn't understand. Shout*
> *out to Lawrence and others for exposing these creeps. I'm*
> *sure it's a lot of us. We've got a weird energy every time*
> *we get around this dude. Definitely homophobic."*

One comment is from one of the people that actually got on the news and said Ola said something homophobic. He said he talked recklessly about homosexuals while he was on set with him for real, for real. Talked recklessly about homosexuals.

What the hell does that mean exactly? It was like everyone had a lie that they would tell to one person, who would tell another and another! Then they would spiral from there! There's nothing like a rumor mill to get a lie out there!

Every day there was a new lie to add fuel to the fire. We had to let these idiots spew their hateful venom and destroy our lives! Mentally it was debilitating! It got to the point where I didn't want to see what was said next! At the same time, social media can be sort of like an addiction, and it is hard not to look. I would think, what else can they say? They have already said it all!

Then I'd find something new I would never have imagined, let alone thought to do but was accused of it in front of the world to see! There was one guy who said he could tell I was gay by the way I shook his hand! What the hell was he smoking? What does a handshake have to do with anything? But he was adamant my handshake said I was gay! I wonder what my right hook would have said?

In the back of my mind, I was wondering where my friend, the man I went clubbing with, the man I believed was more than just a friend. He was more like a brother; I wondered where he was. Why wasn't he defending us? Why wasn't he telling the truth? He wanted publicity to post on social media, but once he got it, he stepped out of the spotlight as soon as the police realized he was playing them! He had sent me this text message.

> *Brother…. I love you. I stand with you. I know 1000% you and your brother did nothing wrong and never would. I am making a statement so everyone else knows. They'll not get away with this. Please hit me when they let you go. I'm behind you fully.*

My life had fallen apart, and people were saying all kinds of shit about me. I had to sit back and let my reputation, my brother's reputation, and my family's reputation all be questioned, and I wasn't allowed to do anything about it. I can't remember a time I was more frustrated in my life! I was in a dark place because I couldn't defend myself. People could just literally say anything, and it was taken as fact about who I was! Half of these people didn't even know me. They just wanted to get in on the lies to get their fifteen minutes of fame!

The more lies told, the more I found myself slipping into that dark place. The only people I was able to defend myself to was my family, the last people I should have had to defend myself to! Gloria would ask me about some stuff because she would hear it and not know if there was any truth in it or not. Some of these things could have been disputed by saying my brother and I never worked on a single episode of *Empire* together! I could easily have dispelled that rumor had I been able to point out we never were on set together, but no!

I got to the point where I would see the new lie and would try to find facts to refute it. If I ever got the chance to, that is! One statement we made through Gloria was that we are American citizens. We do not hate Donald Trump. Of course, that could make some people happy and others sad. Jussie had Ola, and I say, 'This is MAGA country!' Those words and a red hat put the 'attack' on Trump Supporters or haters, depending on who you talk to. Gloria, let us make that statement in hopes some of the lies would stop. How naïve we were.

Ola: I tried not to let the little stuff I saw online bother me. My concern was what I saw on the news. Most reporters on the news don't have snide comments from people to fuel their stories. Most reporters deal in facts. It was those that bothered me. These people were getting their information from lies on social media and reporting it as truth!

I understood why Gloria didn't want us to refute anything. In some way, anything we said could be misconstrued and affect the court case. But at the same time, not being able to defend ourselves, it felt like we were fighting a fight on two fronts. The battle of public opinion versus the court battle. The most important one was the court case.

Until that was dealt with, we had to ignore the shots fired day after day in the media. We let Jussie and his team fight it out in the media. They did a good job, but when it came down to it, we stood alone except in the court. It was what happened in that courtroom that mattered, not what lies the people would believe!

Chapter Nineteen

CHARGES DISMISSED?

Ola: As court approached, we began to hear about a possible leak in the police department. The check was leaked, as well as the video showing Bola and me purchasing the stuff. Originally the deputies had told us the check wouldn't be needed, but they had eventually come to the hotel and asked for it. Bola had to go to the bank with them to get a copy of it. Once the leaks started, we lost all faith in the CPD.

I wasn't sure who to trust anymore. It was like we were being beaten down again and again in the media, and then the police, who are supposed to have our backs, are leaking things to the press. I was over it! Done!

I was beginning to wonder if we would ever see a light at the end of the tunnel! When was this thing going to be over? I wanted my life back! I was tired of being held hostage by this mess! When would life return to normal?

Then I began to think that maybe this was my new normal. I started preparing myself for what was to come mentally. I took to meditating and reading a lot more self-help books and listening to motivational videos, and just trying to keep myself in a good mind space.

After all this upheaval in our lives, the States prosecutor just suddenly dropped the case. No explanation. No apology for wasting CPD's time and resources. No thanks for wasting your time testifying for a grand jury. Not even thanks to the grand jury for wasting their time! Just the charges are dropped!

Jussie was charged with sixteen felony charges, and the grand jury made the decision to indict him. Then Kim Foxx, the State's Attorney, decided Jussie was done wrong and should be free to go. He waved the return of his $10,000.00 bond and supposedly did a few hours of community service.

Ms. Foxx released this statement:

"After reviewing all of the facts and circumstances of the case, including Mr. Smollett's volunteer service in the community and agreement to forfeit his bond to the City of Chicago, we believe this outcome is a just disposition and appropriate resolution to this case."

That's it! In her eyes, Jussie was free and clear!

At the time, Gloria had a PR firm working for her. They wanted us to come out and make a statement saying we supported the CPD and the state's attorney's decision to drop the charges. My brother and I refused. We wanted to wait until we had more information on why the charges were dropped. We supported CPD even though we didn't trust them completely. But the prosecutor was a different story. We knew nothing about her other than she was the one who decided Jussie was the one treated wrong, not us. No way were we going to support anything she said if her stance was that!

The PR firm didn't like that and instructed Gloria to drop us off as clients. I felt like there was a form of betrayal here. We weren't saying we wouldn't make a statement. We just wanted more information. That wasn't asking for too much; we didn't think. Evidently, they did. Gloria took our side in it and fired them!

Jussie didn't have to make a statement or say he was sorry. Just you're free and clear. He actually came out boasting, saying, "I would not be my mother's son if I was capable of one drop of what I was accused with." I thought, what the hell! He was just let go with not even a slap on the wrist! He forfeited his $10,000.00 bond and a few hours of community service. To make matters worse, the files were sealed! Gloria wasn't able to see them either!

While my brother and I had our lives turned upside down, Jussie was free to move on as if nothing had happened. Come to find out, the prosecutor, Ms. Foxx, was friends with Jussie's family! She even texted them while the case was going on! Then she dropped the charges and sealed the files! Even Gloria couldn't see them!

Bola: I was done with everyone! I was skeptical from day one, and that feeling grew as each day passed. With each new lie, I pulled back on who I trusted and with what. If I'm being honest, I was a little wary about trusting Gloria too. Then the PR firm betrays us. They wanted the statement to come out quickly, saying we stand with the CPD, that we told them the truth, and that we stand firm with them. Pretty much, that's what they wanted us to say. But like Ola said, we felt like we were being rushed into the fire, and we didn't know where it was going to take us.

We said we wanted to hold back until we knew more. The case against Jussie had been dropped out of the blue, and we weren't in the loop on why! After the leaks and then the dismissal of charges, we wanted time to regroup and figure out what we wanted to say, not what they wanted us to say. There was also a story in the paper at this time that mentioned fifty Northwestern Hospital employees were fired for sharing Jussie's hospital records with the press.

Jussie was free and clear, while Ola and I were left to get our lives back. The icing on the cake was hearing Jussie had ruined the lives of fifty other people too! I know there are people who would say these people lost their jobs because they chose to sell Jussie's records to the highest bidder. There is truth in that, but if Jussie had never come up with this crazy hoax, none of these people, these first responders, would have been fired!

Shortly after this, Gloria drops us as her clients. At first, we were confused but then realized we were no longer in need of a criminal defense attorney; we never really did. We weren't charged with anything. The media blew her dropping us as clients way out of proportion, trying to make it seem she dropped us because we were guilty or some nonsense!

Gloria then became our attorney in the defamation lawsuit we filed against Jussie's lawyers for lies they told during the course of the investigation. We weren't able to file suit against any of the trolls on social media, but we were able to sue Jussie's attorneys for saying I was in a relationship with Jussie. They also claimed Ola and I wore white face which was a devastating impact on me.

After going through this torturous time, I have learned to stop worrying about what people think of me. If someone wants to say I'm gay, let them. I know I'm not. It doesn't matter what they say; there is no power behind those words that will affect me. I am who I am meant to be! Those who want to ridicule and treat others as if they are inferior to them are the ones that I feel bad for. They are too busy tormenting some poor person for whatever reason because they aren't happy with the person they are. They prefer to make others feel bad to hide their own issues.

Ola: Someone asked me once if, after all the lies and turmoil I faced because of this hoax if at any time I thought I was being accused of it, I might as well just go beat the shit out of Jussie. Even though I am still dealing with the fallout from this incident, I wouldn't go after him. I chose to be the bigger person. He made this mess and pulled my brother and me down with him, but we will climb our way back up! No man has the right to hold me down! The Almighty made me the man I am today!

With the civil suit filed, I expected our lives to go back to normal. I quickly learned I had my expectations too high. I began training people here and there when able. I do online training as well. There has been a little boost in that. People have reached out about me writing them meal plans and workout plans. I have a few clients I train in the gym each week. Slowly I am getting passed this and building my client base.

Bola: Upon being released from jail, I had to get back to training immediately. I was signed up to compete in an annual amateur boxing competition, the Golden Gloves. This is one of the most elite and prestigious amateur tournaments in the country. Great champions have won that tournament, **Muhammad Ali, Sonny Liston,** and **Joe Louis,** just to name a few. And I had just won the Chicago Division the first time I fought. I began my boxing career in December of 2018 and won them just three months later. It was a big deal that I won those fights. At the time, I worked out at Hamlin Park with my coach Bill Heglin for my boxing training. My first competition was on March 14, 2019.

The Golden Gloves was the first time I came out in public since the news had broken. Everyone was crowding us and asking questions. All I wanted was to focus on boxing. I knocked out my opponent with a technical knockout, which meant the referee decided my opponent wasn't fit to continue the fight. I won the senior novice division 178-pound limit match.

I won the Golden Gloves against an opponent who had over ten fights. It was my third fight! He had been boxing for years. I'd been boxing for two months. And I won the Golden Gloves!

That was my first year with the Golden Gloves. I fought against some really amazing boxers. To win, I had to win each fight. I won the following:

- March 14, 2019. The first night of the quarter-finals.
  My opponent: Francisco Mera.
  Total knockout in round one.

- March 21, 2019, First night of semifinals.
  My opponent: Xavier Norals.
  Unanimous in the Senior Novice 178 Division.

- April 12, 2019, The finals.
  My opponent: John Broderick
  Total knockout in round one.

The second year I won because the opponents I pulled were afraid to fight me. I had just won the USA National Championships. I guess they didn't want to face losing against me. Instead, they just forfeited the fight. I can count them as a win, but it's not the same as actually competing and beating my opponent.

It felt good to win and have people looking at me as a winner instead of one of the brothers who faked attacking Jussie. People didn't expect me to win. To me, this was a highlight within all the hell in my life because I chose to help a friend and destroyed my life.

Some people have asked me if I ever thought of Jussie when I fight. If I see his face instead of my opponent's. I don't see his face, but I do have some pent-up frustration over everything. That may come out a little when I box.

When interviewed and the questions went to the 'attack, I was as vague as possible in reply and turned the questions back to the competition and the fact I won it. Most interviewers took the hint!

It was time to begin the next stage in my life, to get my life back on track. What life was like before the incident was gone? We won't ever have that back. We are public images, just not the way we thought it would be.

We have always had the mindset we would make it big. We have prepared for it, but now we just have to navigate it in a totally different way than we had planned. We didn't plan for it to come this fast or in this manner. If not for our inner strength, sense of worth, and knowledge of our royal heritage, we may have removed ourselves from the limelight.

In May 2019, I met my coach, Nate Jones. Nate is Mayweather's best friend/trainer. They were together in the 96 Olympics. Both of them won a bronze medal. At this point, I haven't made much from my boxing, but with him in my corner and my abilities, that will soon change! Meeting him showed me I was going in the direction I was meant to. I also had Jeff Mason as a coach. The belief these two men had in me meant so much to me.

> After Bola's win at the Golden Gloves, Steph Walsh from @WashNews tweeted:
>
> "Tonight at the Chicago Golden Gloves Finals— Abimbola "Abel" Osundairo overpowered his opponent from the start.
>
> After the match he told me he's just boxing for fun, training 5 days a week.
>
> Tonight was all about his win; he didn't want to discuss anything else.

Chapter Twenty

PSYCH, JUST KIDDING!

Ola: When we are finally seeing an end to the madness, word of a special prosecutor being hired to reevaluate the case comes. I was happy to hear about it but annoyed a little too. I dreaded what was to come. We would have a chance to clear our names. Finally!

After the charges had been dropped, I thought it wasn't going to be possible. I didn't think it was an option. When I heard that there was a special prosecutor and that they were reopening the case again, I was very excited. But at the same time, I was like, here we go again. Time for the spotlight to be on us again. What fresh hell would come our way this time?

As with every moment of my life, not just when it is in turmoil, I rely on my faith to keep me together. Through my faith, I am able to stay positive about everything. I know that whatever happens to me is happening for a reason. I know God has a plan for everything. I trust in Him, in my faith, and I know that He will get me through whatever situation I am in. That's what really kept me strong and together through everything and what continues to get me through life today.

Bola: I'm not going to lie; when the case was thrown out against Jussie, I thought, damn, he must know some powerful people. I had seen all the conspiracy theories about him being related to the Obamas or Vice President Kamala Harris. When the case was dropped, I assumed that must be true. If not them, some other powerful people.

I could feel myself sinking into that dark place. With no case, would we ever have our names cleared? The police knew it was faked. Close family and friends knew it was fake and that we'd been doing it for a friend. But what about the public? Their opinion mattered. They were the ones who would decide if we were clear to go back to our lives or if we would forever have this hanging over our heads because the truth wasn't out there.

I know there are still people who believe Jussie to this day. But there were some who wanted to know if there was any truth in the rumors about us. If Jussie would just admit he had planned the whole thing and asked us to do it because we were friends who would do what we could to help a friend, all the negative media would fade away.

I wasn't even in America on August 23rd, 2019, when I received word from the Judge…what was his name…Michael Toomin appointed Dan Webb as the special prosecutor to determine if there were charges to file against Jussie. I didn't know what to expect. I had no idea what a special prosecutor was supposed to do. I found out later this prosecutor, Dan Webb, was independent of any office. His sole purpose was to go through the grand jury's indictment and see if charges needed to be filed. Again.

At this point, the police and the legal system weren't exactly winning me over! Between tossing the case out without making Jussie admit his hand in this and the leaks, and Tina Glandian's white face comment, they weren't exactly batting a thousand!

Once I knew what Mr. Webb was doing, I just waited to see how it played out while going about my life with any and everything that had nothing to do with Jussie Smollett!

I could feel myself slipping toward that dark place. I turned to my faith and prayed, asking for guidance and help to pull me from the mouth of the dark place. After being in jail and facing all of the betrayal, Ola and I went to church. It wasn't on a Sunday, as we weren't there to disrupt the service, and at that time, with all going on, our presence probably would. We met with the pastor and a few others, and they prayed for us and did a little ceremony for us. My faith has always been powerful. Nothing could ever make me doubt or question my faith!

I was in Nigeria for the first time since the incident. I didn't see a lot of people one on one while there, as I was there to train. I wanted to get in a little practice before I went to qualify for the African Games. The games are a multi-sport event from all nations of Africa. This was a big deal for me and Nigeria. I was there to represent my heritage, my culture, for Nigeria. Unfortunately, I ended up not participating in the games. I was in a match that I won, but it was given to my opponent. Nigeria, like everywhere, has politics that must be catered to. I chose not to compete as a result.

I wasn't there just for the games. I was also there, as one of the members of Team Abel, sponsoring a free medical event in front of our home, God's Grace. Unfortunately, Ola wasn't able to be there with me. We had nurses, doctors, medicine, and water. Everything was free to those in need. One thing people don't know about us is we are humbled to be able to help others. To reach out to them and assist them in any way. This event was but one way we helped our community. We offer what we can and throw in some love on the side with a touch of positive energy!

Community, like family, is very important to us. We hope to unite Africa. For now, we do what we can to help those in need. This event was more than just free medical help; it was a time to come together as a community and feel the love and support of those around you. Everything was free. If your blood pressure was checked and a doctor said it was high and gave you a prescription, it was filled before you left. If your sugar was bad, the same thing happened. Just because our lives were a mess didn't mean we were going to tuck our tails in and run! There were more than three thousand people show up that day. The community came together as one. God's Grace was there within every man, woman, and child!

Our goal was to target those at risk of hypertension which is a common risk factor for chronic kidney disease, heart failure, and strokes among Nigerian adults. We hope to make this event happen again.

Before heading for America, I had a chance to create a track while there. It is sort of like an afro beast song. Music is something Ola, and

I want to get into. We've done a few songs and plan to do more in the future as the Nigerian Brothers.

Ola: Gloria was the one who let me know about Dan Webb and what he would be doing. I didn't want to go through the process, but I knew I had to if we were ever going to get our names cleared. I wasn't looking forward to having to go downtown. Downtown meant getting an Uber because there's no parking down there. I knew I would lose most of the day, possibly more, spending hours going over what happened again. I had sat with the prosecutor the first time around and knew how long it had taken. There would be pretrial prep, and that took hours!

I was about 80% sure I wanted to do all this again. The other 20% of me was over it! I wanted my name and my brother's name cleared, but the media circus that would come from this was enough to make me have a few thoughts saying don't get into this again! Things were beginning to improve. I had clients again. I could see the sky again instead of being bogged down in the weeds. And then this happened!

Mr. Webb met with Jussie and us first. I told him my story, and Bola told him his. Then he spoke with Jussie. After that, the evidence was gone through; a decision was made to indict Jussie again. Now it is a waiting game. How long before the trial?

As the trial date approached, Jussie hired Nenye Uche as his lawyer. Back in the beginning, before Gloria became our lawyer, this Uche guy had tried to get us to have him as our lawyer. Gloria and Mr. Webb wanted him thrown off the case. Suddenly we were on a side mission with the court. My mother was brought in and had to explain how Nenye Uche had approached us prior to the first grand jury. It was definitely a conflict of interest, we said.

Nenye Uche claimed he didn't speak with us, and therefore nothing had been told to him about the case. A family friend had given him our contact, and we had spoken on the phone; we had cell phone records to prove it. He had spoken to my mother as well, which was why she had to speak to the prosecutor. The judge ruled he could remain on Jussie's team but wasn't able to cross-examine Bola or me.

Bola: We were still missing some of our confiscated items by the police from the first go around. When I was arrested at the airport, I had a painting I had picked up in Nigeria.

There was $700 taken from the house when the police executed their search warrant while we were in lockup. That money is still missing. We have asked about it, but we were told something about the FBI having it. At this point, I doubt we will ever get any of it back. And here we were, opening our lives up again. At least this time, there wouldn't be another search of our stuff being gone through and kept again.

We were beginning to build our lives back, and now a trial was looming once again. I won boxing match after match, and Ola was training again. This new trial was great if it meant our names were to be cleared and Jussie was to be held accountable for what happened! But I couldn't help wondering how this would affect our lives and careers this time. Things were finally on track! Money wasn't great, but we at least had some coming in. This trial couldn't interfere with that. It took forever to get jobs last time!

Ola: This time around, I was more prepared. I had kind of an idea of how things would go. There were stories about Bola being gay and going to a bathhouse with Jussie. Bola did go with him, but not as Jussie's lover, as Jussie's friend. It didn't faze me as much this time. I guess because these same lies were told before.

Bola: *The New York Post* put out an article about me being a disgruntled lover, and that was the reason I 'attacked' Jussie. I wasn't allowed to defend myself. Once it was said in one post or article, it would be posted everywhere online.

I would see my own friends on social media take the post and update their status with it like they believed the lies. I wanted so badly to ask them what the hell! Friends didn't do that! If you ever want to know who your true friends are, have something like this happen. The true ones will be those who have your back! The ones that post the lies are the ones you need to kick to the curb!

I am a strong man; I would never let anything like this break me. Seeing people I thought were my friends doing this so they would have their posts go viral pissed me off! I used my faith to keep me from going off on them.

Ola: My belief in God was the strength I needed when things got hard. I would not let this incident have me broken down and weak. If the death of my grandparents hadn't broken me, no way would I let this do so! The only time I went down on my knees was to pray.

Before the trial, we had to go downtown to Dan Webb's office. He and his partner, Sam Mendenhall, prepared us for how the trial would go from direct examination questions to cross-examination questions. They did a pretty good job preparing us for what Jussie's lawyers would do. It took hours, but there was one thing I could say about this prosecutor and his partner. They were not willing to lose! They knew something had gone wrong the first time around, and they wanted to make sure Jussie paid for his crime instead of a slap on the wrists and release.

Tunji Adebayo Foundation is but one foundation that
Team Abel is proud to assist.

Chapter Twenty-One

WHAT HE SAID

Bola: I was in Atlanta training and sparring with other fighters to get ready for a boxing tournament, the USA National Championship, scheduled from December 5-11 in Shreveport, LA. This tournament is the highest level of boxing in America. I was a bit nervous going to that tournament because I didn't know if I would have to be in court.

If I could skip court and just go to the fight, I would have. I told them they needed to call me to testify first. It couldn't conflict with my match; if it did, I was going to my match. I told them ahead of time. This match was about my future! Court was about my past!

I was scheduled first because of my schedule but also because it started with me. On my first day in court, I do my morning ritual. I say the Lord's Prayer. Then I do my affirmations! 'I am the greatest universal, renowned speaker, leader, boxer, actor, and thinker to have ever graced this universe. Glory be to the Almighty. What the Almighty brings together, nothing can take apart.' Then I sit and meditate and breathe in and out. I hold my breath a little bit as I breathe deep and then release. This is my morning ritual every morning. I didn't eat breakfast because I didn't want to feel lethargic. I didn't want to be like that on the stand.

I began doing my voice and facial exercises. I would go, "Aaaaaaa. Ooooooo. Eeeeeee. Iiiiiii. Uuuuuuu. I was getting myself ready to talk to people. This was something actors did. We met at Popeyes, as Gloria requested, we prayed together and then went to the courthouse. Media swarmed us, but we paid them no mind. I was shown to a room to wait until it was my time to testify. I didn't have to wait too long.

As I walked past those people in the courtroom, I felt all their eyes on me. I felt like I had better not screw up with all these people watching. For four hours, I sat there answering all the questions thrown at me in direct examination. Occasionally I was asked to point out something on a screen. I had to show how we walked around from one area to the next on a map. I made sure to keep eye contact with different members of the jury when I answered. I made sure to look at whoever was asking me a question before looking at the jury to answer. Eye contact is polite when talking to someone.

The cross-examination was almost like one of my sparring matches. They would throw a punch, and I would counter with the truth. I was asked why I would do this in the middle of a polar vortex. It was minus twenty, and I was waiting to attack Jussie. Why else would I be out there at that time of night in such freezing temperatures? They thought that punch would hit me, but I blocked it. I told them I was out at that time of night in that freezing weather to help a friend by making the 'fake attack' he had orchestrated.

I was taught to never reply in anger. As a result, I take a moment when someone asks or says something and think about my response before going off hot-headed. This was something I think the defense was hoping I would do. They thought they could taunt me, and I would snap in anger. They quickly saw that wasn't happening! I think this aggravated them, but I think the jury could tell what they were doing. There were a couple of questions filled with the lies the media had heard. I think they thought that would have me snapping at them as we hadn't been able to refute them, but I thought first and then answered calmly. My eyes were on the jury as I did.

The truth was on my side, so I didn't have to keep lies straight. That's the way it is when you lie. Jussie should have realized that. Once the lie is told, you have to tell the same lie to the next person and the next, and so on and so forth, until the truth comes out. I was telling the truth, so for every punch they swung my way, I blocked or ducked completely.

Even when they tried to trip me up by saying something I had said but altering it to sound bad, I didn't let that punch land. They made me a little uncomfortable with their hostility, but I had the truth on my side. When I left that day, I knew I could count this as a win. The question was would the jury do so?

One of the officials for the boxing championship emailed me. He basically said he knew what I was going through, and if I wanted to cancel, that would be fine. They wanted to make sure my head was in the game. I emailed back, saying hell no, I would be there! I was coming! Not to worry about it; my head would be in the match and nothing else! They gave me a late check-in so I could testify first. I was thankful they were willing to work with me.

Ola: When the day of the trial arrives, I am more than ready! I don't eat breakfast as I only eat once a day. I didn't want to feel sluggish or anything. Once dressed, I go through my morning affirmations before I get ready to head out to court. They wanted me there two hours before court began. This is my morning routine, anyway. Today I just take a little more time doing it.

My morning affirmations are important to me. I took a deep breath and said, 'Binjo, you are a child of God. Binjo, you are great. Binjo, you are awesome. Binjo, you are an excellent dancer. Binjo, you are number one. Binjo, you are on top. Bingo, you're successful. Binjo, you will succeed. Binjo, you will be prosperous. Binjo, you are wealthy. Binjo, you are healthy. Binjo, you will win. Binjo, you are handsome. Binjo, people want to do for you. Binjo, people want to give you opportunities. Binjo, you are loved. Binjo, you are wanted. Binjo, you are the man.'

I called an Uber and started running some of the questions. I am mentally preparing myself for the questions I will be asked. I also prepared my voice. I did my vowels the way my brother did, preparing my voice and facial muscles for my testimony.

As Bola said, Gloria wanted us to meet at the Popeyes next door to the courthouse so we could walk together to the courthouse. She knew the media would surround us the moment we got close to the courthouse. My mom was there, as well as two friends of mine, to do security for us.

Moving through the media took a few minutes. Inside we had to go into separate rooms where the witnesses waited until they called us to testify.

Bola had testified the day before, and he said things went well. It was boring sitting there waiting my turn. I was ready for this to be over with. The two hours I sat in that room felt like an eternity. After two years of my life, I was ready to be done with this! Permanently! The prosecutor had done a good job on the questions he expected. Though not as many as we expected to be asked. I was on the stand for less than two hours.

The cross-examination by Jussie's attorney was argumentative. They were hostile, but it was covered well with their demeanor. I could tell Jussie's attorneys were getting angry. They couldn't trip me up. And they tried. Often. They complained to the judge. For every question they asked, I faced the jury and answered them. You are supposed to look at the person you are talking to. That shouldn't change just because I was talking to twelve people.

The attorneys were almost comical in the way they behaved. One of them said the judge even lunged at her. All I could think was, Jussie is paying a lot of money for this? It appeared as if they had prepared the night before. It almost looked like they didn't do their homework the night before and were trying to make it up as they went. These people went to school for this! Like they really went to school for this! I could have done a better job.

I think Jussie's whole family was in the courthouse, the whole entourage. They were all looking at me like I did something wrong. I guess, in their eyes, I had. I doubt Jussie told them the truth. I smiled at them. I didn't really give them any negative type of energy. I smiled at them all the time. I had no reason to give off negative energy; I hadn't done anything to worry about. As was becoming apparent to them with each passing moment. Not that they would admit that!

Bola: The minute my testimony was over, I was on a plane to Shreveport, LA. I had to sign in and then check in as the tournament was beginning. Usually, when going to a match, the fighter has to have a coach in their corner. Someone who will wrap your hands to make sure they are wrapped correctly. If not, you can do serious damage to your hands. I had to find someone to be my coach. At times Ola has been in my corner, but for this tournament, I had to find someone.

I was so grateful it worked out. I was late for the boxing tournament. I was supposed to get there on the fifth, I think, but I had to stay for court another day.

There was a father and son; the son was competing, whom I had met in Atlanta when I was training and sparring. I asked them if they would be in my corner on the day of my first fight when I was getting my gloves and gear. The father had said he would, but when the time came, neither answered my call!

I was getting anxious! No coach meant no fight. I didn't want to be disqualified! The time to complete it was getting closer, and I was starting to worry and get anxious. There is no one to wrap my hands or be in my corner! I broke my hand once because I my hands hadn't been properly wrapped by a coach. I need someone who could wrap them and do so now, as that takes some time.

Instead of getting ready for the fight, I ran around asking different people if they could help me. Everyone was saying no, as they had their own fighters. Finally, I found two gentlemen who would help me wrap my hands and stay in my corner. They stayed for two days, but then they had to travel. I was thankful for the time they gave me! They really helped me! I had another man help me in my corner for the next two days.

I had coaches that would have been there for me if we had been absolutely certain I would make the tournament. It was $1000 to get to Shreveport. No one wanted to pay that in case, at the last minute, I would be stuck doing something for the trial. I couldn't call them last minute and say I'm on a plane; meet me there. The ticket was even more expensive last minute. I did finally see the father and son. They didn't explain what happened, but he ended up losing, so it didn't really matter. I may have been running around right before the match, but I won it!

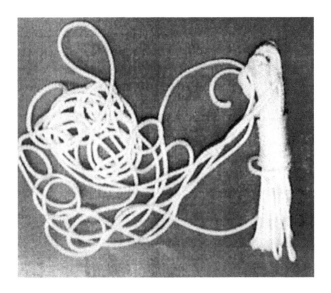

The rope the 'attackers' were accused of putting around Jussie's neck.

The bottle the 'attackers' had the bleach in.

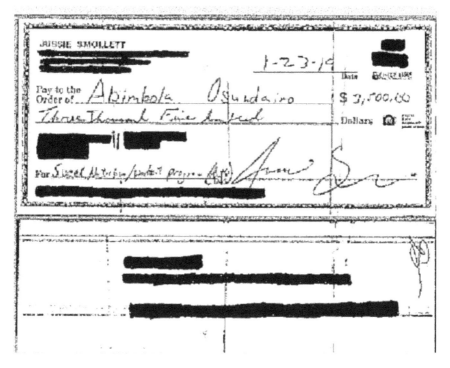

The Check that Jussie paid the brothers with.

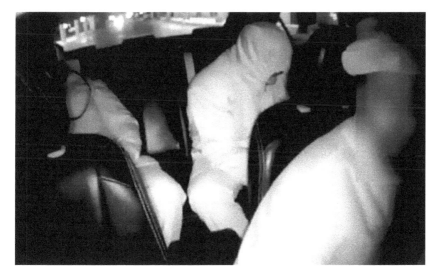

The brothers on their way to the scene of the 'attack' in costume.

Chapter Twenty-Two

GUILTY OR INNOCENT?
THAT IS THE QUESTION

Ola: The day of the verdict, I was a little nervous. I knew my brother, and I had nothing to be nervous about, but twelve people may believe Jussie's lies. All it took was one for this to go downhill. Gloria told me Jussie did a good job when he was on the stand.

My mother, Gloria, her PA Sandy, and two of my security were in the overflow room where we could watch a TV to see the proceedings. There were three or so other people in the room that were for Jussie. I could tell because they kept giving me dirty looks. I wasn't supposed to be on my phone, but I was, and they kept telling the courthouse security I was. They were acting like spoiled brats!

I went through the what-ifs while I sat in that room waiting for the verdict. Suppose they found Jussie innocent; that would have people questioning Bola's and my character. Our name would be sullied forever. Could the jury truly believe my brother and I was capable of attacking someone?

Would the police try to come after us if Jussie was cleared? My mind was running through every scenario. The jury deliberated for nine hours over two days. I had plenty of time to go over the different possibilities the verdict could bring. December 10, 2021, they found him guilty! It was like a weight had been lifted off my shoulders.

When the verdict came down, they were not happy, Jussie's followers! One of them came over and put a note in my hand, and walked off. It said:

> *I know CPD forced you and set you*
> *up. The attackers were two white*
> *men, with another one involved.*
> *3 total. There are videos.*
> *Please tell the truth.*
> *Please tell the truth.*
> *If you don't, how will things*
> *ever change in Chicago?*

At first, I laughed. She had to be joking! How could she believe the 'attackers' were white? Had she not listened to anything about the trial? I showed my mom. She was surprised too. I felt sorry for them in a way; these people didn't know him. They were fans, and because he was a celebrity, there was no way he was lying. At least, that is what I would guess is a reason.

They believe wholeheartedly Jussie was not involved. I know some of it may stem from a lack of trust in the Chicago Police Department. I understand the CPD does have a reputation that my brother and I had nothing to do with, but I can see why people would hold them accountable if they truly believed Jussie's lies. I had my own issues with CPD after the leaks!

I had driven that day. Gloria made a statement to the media, pointing out that Bola couldn't be there with us because he was at a boxing event. She mentioned our mother had flown in from Nigeria to be with us. She thanked everyone for helping us to be heard. She knew there would be a lot of questions left unanswered by this, but she wouldn't take questions. She actually wished Jussie well in a roundabout way. She asked him to see how our lives had turned around and that he could hopefully do the same to his.

Gloria has been a blessing! I bet she never thought when she handed my mother her card that one day she would be assisting in the weirdest hoax the world has ever seen. We can't begin to thank her enough for her support and guidance. She is family now. She couldn't get rid of us if she wanted to. She told the press and the world that when the time was right, we would tell the what, the why, and the how.

On the way home, I was kind of nervous. I wasn't sure what to expect now that this was finally over. I found myself checking behind me as if someone might be following us. Earlier in the trial, I had seen someone following me. I guess that was what had me thinking someone might be following me that day. I drove around a little before actually going home.

Bola: I fought matches four days in a row, and I won the USA National Championship! This was a major win! I was #1 in the US! After all, I had gone through to be there to fight and then the last-minute need for a coach, I had come out first! While I was there, I got the news that Jussie had been found guilty! I counted that as a win, thankful the truth had prevailed!

A weight lifted from my shoulders. Finally, this was done! Jussie was found guilty! Everyone now knew he had been behind the entire thing! But Jussie hadn't admitted it. He still denied it. I could have let that bother me and overshadow my achievements that day, but I refused to let another minute of Jussie's mess interfere with my life!

People will believe what they want to believe. I can't change that. I no longer worry about that. Believe me and my brother, or believe Jussie. That is your choice, but it doesn't affect me. I know the truth, as does my brother and Jussie though he won't admit it!

The win against Jussie meant now I could concentrate on my life and what I wanted to do with it. I was #1 in America, and I found myself on the US Olympic Boxing Team! I had been boxing for two years, and I was on the Olympic Team! That was exhilarating to know I was #1 while still having my life dominated by the incident!

When I got home, my brother and I went to the place where his girlfriend worked and had a homecoming celebration. They played the Queen song: *We Are the Champions* as I entered with my belt. I was wearing a red trucker hat with MAGA on it; only the first A was replaced with the African continent. It meant Make Africa Great Again. TMZ captured it all on video. They seemed to be the ones who covered this incident the most. If something happened, they were usually the ones first reporting it. I'm not sure if they are just that good or if they were stalkers. Either way, it would be out for the world to see in a matter of minutes.

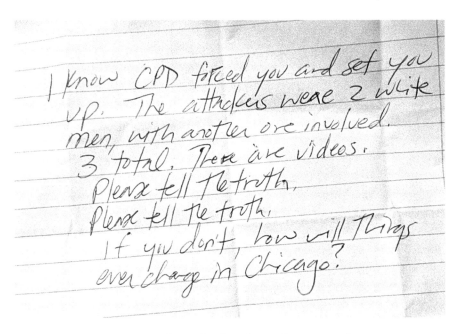

Note passed to Ola after the verdict was read.

Chapter Twenty-Three

THEY WERE KIDNAPPED BY ALIENS

Ola: With the guilty verdict, I had hoped people would finally know Jussie was behind the whole thing, but sadly there are still people to this day, who believe Jussie was not involved in his 'attack.' These people almost blindly follow him as if he is some sort of savior or something. There are so many conspiracy theories I can't keep up!

One theory that sort of goes along with the note I mentioned before, there are three white guys; one was off camera as you only see two figures running. I don't know where this guy was supposed to have gone, but there are people who honestly think there is another man out there who got away with it completely, as he was never seen on camera!

There is the theory my brother and I made the 'attack,' and there was a third guy who was white. After all, the Uber and the cab drivers both said there was at least one white guy. This is obviously not a good theory as there are only two people in the cab and Uber. Where do they think the third person was? In the trunk? Tied to the top? Maybe he was on the hood acting as the hood ornament.

The theory of the third person seems to be very popular. This theory is one where there are three white men, and the CPD is involved in helping us to cover up his existence while lying and framing Jussie. Supposedly in this theory, the CPD has something they are holding over our heads, making us lie and point the finger at Jussie!

I have no idea which is dumbest, that these people think we are career criminals with lots of crimes to be blackmailed with or thinking a cop would want to hold something over our heads so we could 'frame' Jussie. Do these people seriously think the Chicago Police Department gives a shit about what Jussie does as long as it's legal? I think this may be the stupidest!

Apparently, a lot of these theories center around the disgruntled lover angle. As the theory goes, I found out Bola and Jussie were lovers. And to prove to me he wasn't, I made Bola attack him. Someone, please explain to me how this is even a theory! So, if he beats up Jussie, that's supposed to be proof to me that he's not gay? Why would that be proof? Honestly, these conspiracy nuts need to really give these things more thought.

I think the strangest one is that we 'beat' him up because we wanted him to hire us as his security. The logic there is beyond me! These aren't the worst! There are so many more! At this point, I ignore them all! Some people just need to get a life and learn to let shit go!

Bola: After winning the USA National Championship, I went to Springfield, MA, for a training camp. There was a coach there who was to train with me and spar. He then introduced me to another manager. At this time, I am looking to turn professional. I was there about a week before being invited into the OTC, the Olympic Training Center, in Colorado Springs, Colorado.

I was invited, and Ola went with me. I went there to train with the US Olympic Team. It was amazing! I got massages every day because they looked after their athletes. We ate well; they had a cafeteria where we got three meals a day and snacks between if we wanted them.

It was awesome being at a big training center. We worked out twice a day, and if we wanted to, we were able to work out more. It is a different kind of energy there. Everyone around you is good, maybe as good as you are. This is the best of the best, the US Olympic Team! It wasn't just the boxers; this training center is for all US Olympic Teams. Swimmers, bicyclist, wrestlers, and every athletic group was there with our training. The atmosphere was one of belonging. No matter the sport, we were all there to be on the USA Olympic Team!

I have always known I would be great at everything I did. This is my mindset each day. I tell myself in my affirmations how my life is meant to be. I was twenty-eight and on the Olympic Team!

I wanted to go professional. To do that, I had to wait until I would have gone to the 2024 Olympics. I had a goal that required turning pro now, not in a year or so. As honored as I was to be on a team with all these top-rate athletes, turning pro is a new thing. I walked away from the team. I had to do what was best for my overall goal. I know it sounds crazy; this is what people strive for. Now is my time to turn pro and show the world what I can do!

Ola: Until the sentencing, cameras hadn't been allowed in the court-room. Bola wasn't there; he was in New Orleans for a fight. March 10, 2022, Jussie was sentenced to 150 days in Cook County Jail. He was on a thirty-month felony probation that he will serve in that court. He was to pay $120,106.00 restitution to the city of Chicago. The judge also gave him the max fine of $25,000.00. That was nothing to Jussie!

I must admit I was a little surprised by the sentencing. I wouldn't wish a day in jail on anyone, let alone 150. To be honest, I was surprised at the number of charges. What he did was wrong. He did choose to lie to the police and cause a whole lot of people to waste their time, but wasn't that a little extreme?

But then I thought about how my brother and I had our lives flipped upside down because we helped a friend who chose to lie to us and the police. He had shown no remorse about how he disrupted mine or Bola's life. The charges were justified!

Not only was he found guilty, but the judge also ripped him a new one! He called Jussie out on how he had done everything but didn't stop there. He pointed out that Jussie repeatedly sat on that stand and perjured himself over and over while sticking to his lie! That judge was pissed! For a moment, I felt bad about it…but it quickly passed!

Jussie spouted off some nonsense about how he wasn't lying and said multiple times he wasn't suicidal! Of course, he wasn't! He isn't a martyr. He wouldn't have broken a nail deliberately!

Bola: The sentencing was surprising. When I think about what Jussie said when he asked me to do this and then what he did after I did what he asked, I am torn on his punishment. My life and my brothers were on an upward tick when a friend appealed to me for help.

Not once when Jussie asked this of me did I think he would turn this into the circus he did. I thought his words as he was escorted from the courtroom odd. He proclaimed he was not suicidal. Not once did he apologize for causing so much unnecessary police work. In his mind, he was sticking to his 'script,' and therefore, he believed he had nothing to apologize for.

Looking back at it now, there are so many holes in his plan. One of which is the camera. He pointed out the one that would catch everything for his social media, but the camera faced the other way. Shouldn't he have known that? How was he going to get the video off the camera? It is a privately owned camera. I guess he would have just asked the owner and paid them, if need be, to get it. When someone is filming something for social media, there is usually someone there to film it. If I had thought about these things beforehand, I wonder if Jussie would have had an answer for each concern. Probably!

Chapter Twenty-Four

BUT HE'S A CELEBRITY

Ola: By reporting the 'attack' as a hate crime, Jussie had to know the reaction that would cause in the world. Not just a homophobic hate crime, but a race one as well. These types of crimes are happening everywhere. There has been an uptick in them over the last few years. I think, looking back, Jussie was hoping to have as big of a reaction to his as had been to other recent race crimes.

One of the things that bothered me and my brother about this was how everyone quickly jumped on the hate crime. By that, I mean they didn't wait to hear the details. Someone said a black gay man was attacked by two white southern men, and immediately racial and gay groups began to form protests. I have protested myself for many of these issues.

What bothered me about this was once word got out that my brother and I were the two 'southern white men' the activist took up for Jussie and not us. Black Lives Matter made comments about support for him. But not once was there a moment of support for us when the hoax was revealed. It was almost like we were black, but we weren't celebrity black, so that meant we weren't a part of the Black Lives Matter family. To this day, that organization has not apologized or said anything about us and how we were done. Didn't our black lives matter?

Bola: Honestly, I half expected Jussie to use his time in jail to make out like he had been arrested and was innocent, and then when he got out of jail, I thought he would claim to be like…like he was Mandela, wrongly imprisoned. I could even envision it in my head, him coming out through that gate after his 150 days are up with his hand held high and saying, 'I was falsely imprisoned! I am a prisoner of white supremacy, but I won't let them keep me down! I will rise up and show my oppressors they can't keep this black gay man down!' I could see him finding a way to turn this around and make it benefit him. Hell, he would probably earn an Emmy for it!

I could see all these celebrities writing letters to him about how he was innocent! Demanding the government release him or something! I could imagine the posts on Instagram and Twitter. All the red carpets have that one question asked to each celebrity, 'Do you have anything to say to Jussie?' and celebrity after celebrity saying things like, 'We are praying for your release, Jussie' or 'Be strong, Jussie, we are behind you!'

Thankfully, none of that will happen. As someone who thought of him as a brother, not just a friend, I did feel a moment or two of dismay at the sentence. I spent two days in a cell waiting. I can't imagine what 150 days will be like! I never want to find out! I could have stayed quiet, and maybe he wouldn't have gone to jail, but I had to do what was right for me and my brother. In the same way, Jussie no doubt did what he thought was right for him and his career.

Then I think about how he used me. Looking back on it now, I see it. At the time, I was blind to it. I was enjoying the partying, and doors being opened by being his friend. I don't know if Jussie intended for it to get so out of hand, but by reporting it to the police, how could he not have known something would happen?

I heard one time that a member of the police department said they never said Jussie was guilty. We, the Osundairo brothers, said he was. And the evidence supported that.

Chapter Twenty-Five

AND THE OSCAR GOES TO…

Bola: Jussie took the stand and put on a performance meant to convince everyone he had truly been attacked in a racial and hate crime. He swore to tell the truth before sitting down and proceeded to do the opposite.

His lawyers asked him about the attack being fake.

Jussie said, "There was no hoax." He swore he would never fake a hate crime. He was calm, never angering, regardless of who was asking and what they were asking.

Ola: He swore the check he had written us was for nutrition and training advice, not for a hoax! He repeated there was 'no hoax.' He denied giving us the $100 to pay for the supplies, the props, for the fake 'attack.'

Jussie's story as he returned from a trip and was walking home after buying a sandwich around two in the morning. Someone yelled homophobic and racial slurs at him. He confronted the one who said it. He showed everyone in the courtroom how the attacker had come up behind him and hit him in the temple.

Bola: I didn't hit him there.

Ola: Jussie said on the stand we found out later, 'I would like to think I landed a punch. But I don't know if it landed.'

Bola: He didn't land a punch, but per his instructions, I made it look like he did.

Jussie said he and his attacker slipped and then tussled for a few seconds before he noticed the second attacker. He thinks the second one kicked him before running away. How do you not know if you've been kicked or not?

Bola: A valid question that no one asked. Just one of many!

Jussie 'assumed' the people 'attacking' him were white because one of them said, 'This is MAGA country!' which, as everyone knows, was President Trump's slogan, Make America Great Again. When word of the 'attack' was first getting around, the man himself, President Trump, weighed in on the situation. A member of the press at the White House asked him about the attack. He said, "It doesn't get worse, as far as I'm concerned."

Ola: After the 'attack,' Jussie said he picked up his phone and told whoever was on the other side he had 'got jumped.' It wasn't until he was on the way home with the sub that he hadn't dropped while being 'jumped' that he realized he had a noose around his neck.

Bola: As a black man, how do you not notice a noose around your neck?

Ola: Especially if you are the one who put it there in the first place! I didn't get the noose on him before I saw the lights and took off!

Jussie testified he removed the noose, but his friend at the apartment told him to put it back on so the police officers could see it.

No way would I have done that!

Bola: Supposedly, it was that friend who called the police that he didn't want him to. Jussie's reasoning was because "I am a black man in America. I do not trust the police. I am also a well-known figure at that time, and I am an openly gay man."

I am supposed to believe he didn't call the cops. There is no way the police would be involved if Jussie didn't want them to be. This friend that called the police was one of his managers. If he didn't want the police involved, Jussie would have admitted the truth to his manager. If he didn't want to do that, he could have just forbidden the man to call. After all, the man worked for him. He would have done what Jussie wanted. If Jussie hadn't stopped the call, he should have at least told the truth when they arrived! He wanted the police to see this as a crime.

He actually had the nerve to say he had lost his livelihood!

Ola: He lost his livelihood! What about us? He had money to fall back on! My brother and I had nothing! Our savings were very little. Had our parents not helped where they could, I don't know what we would have done. Eating at a food pantry was just one of the things we had to do to survive. Bola and I have always tried to give back. We don't have much, but we try to help those we can. This was one time when we needed help. Thankfully we had somewhere to turn.

When he was under cross-examination, Jussie was asked why he didn't hand over his phone when the police asked for it. His 'reason' was he wanted privacy. Privacy! Was he serious? Why did he deserve privacy when we had none?

Bola: He had the nerve to say I had mentioned an herbal steroid that helped with weight loss that was illegal in the United States. I had supposedly mentioned this 'on the low' as something I could get in Nigeria.

I have no idea what he is talking about! A steroid shot that helps lose weight! Was he kidding? If something like that existed, I wouldn't have any clients!

This was his reasoning for the text I had testified about that he'd wanted to meet 'on the low' to tell me about the hoax!

He actually testified when he was straight-up asked if he recruited me for a hoax; he said, "Fully false, 100% false."

Jussie said we met at a club in 2017, and he learned we worked to-gether on Empire. We supposedly did drugs together. There were times I would get him the drugs he wanted because he was new to Chicago and wasn't sure of the safe places to get them. I wasn't a dealer; I don't sell drugs.

He then said we went to a bathhouse together where we 'made out' and eventually had a sexual relationship! Was he incapable of telling any of the truth?

The man had the audacity to say that I made him think we needed to 'sneak off' to be together around my brother. He knew my brother, and I were close. He took that and made it twisted to fit his lie! To make everyone think my brother was keeping us from being together! What was keeping us from being together was me! And the fact that I am straight!

I am a nice-looking man, as is my brother. I can see why any gay man would want me, but I don't swing that way.

He swore to tell the truth and has yet to do so! His testimony was full of lies but told with absolute calm. It was as if he believed his lies. Maybe he had himself convinced it was true.

One thing I can say with absolute certainty is Jussie can act! Somebody should call the Academy and nominate him for an Oscar!

Chapter Twenty-Six

IT'S A BOMB!

Ola: There are so many ways this incident could have played out. At the time, my brother and I didn't think about what would happen after the 'attack.' As we have said, this was a role, a gig. Jussie, Bola, and I never talked about Jussie putting the video on social media or anything else. My part was done. For me, that was it.

Bola: I didn't think life would be any different. I helped a friend with a gig, then went on with my life. I expected, upon returning from Nigeria, my life to continue as it had. Boxing, auditions, and hanging out with friends with Jussie. That's what no one understands. This was a gig. Once my part was done, I was on to the next part of my life.

Ola: Unfortunately, that wasn't what happened. We went from four to five auditions a week to none!

Bola: That was when our Talent Agency dropped us. It just was one thing we faced after this incident.

Ola: There seemed to be an increase in appointments for fitness and meal plans, but that turned out to be reporters looking for a quote from the 'attackers.'

Bola: Our lives got ripped apart, many would say, from our own doing, but Jussie, my friend, was looking like a victim! He knew the 'attack' was a hoax! We had performed exactly like his 'script' had said. Right down to my sending what Jussie had requested as a condolence text.

Bruh, say it ain't true. I'm praying for a speedy recovery.

Yet Jussie repeatedly denied it was a hoax. The only thing he said about my brother and I being suspects was, It couldn't be us because we were 'Black as sin'; those were his words. In a text he sent to me, he said, "I know 1000% you and your brother did nothing wrong and never would." That was it! He had plenty of opportunities to say it was a hoax for the world to hear on a daily basis, and that was all he said! All those reporters sticking microphones in his face, and he couldn't manage to say anything about being sorry he had turned our world upside down!

As I saw him continually lie, I realized he was a supervillain. Honestly, it was like I never knew him. Had he only acted like we were friends? How long had he been thinking this scheme up? Had that 'threatening' letter been the cause of Jussie's coming up with this scheme? The FBI isn't sure yet who sent the letter. Could he have sent it to himself? If I'd been asked that question before this, I would have said no. Now, I'm not so sure.

Asking Jussie is out of the question. I had many questions but knew I'd never get any answers. The man has yet to admit it was a hoax! He never will. I truly believe, at this point, Jussie will never admit the truth. He may never, but at least the truth is out for everyone to see.

So many people tweeted support for him. Thousands, maybe millions of people. From celebrities to politicians and everyone in between wanted to show their support for him. He knew reporting the attack as a racial crime would cause a public outcry on race issues. But he claimed it was a hate crime as well! That was like adding fuel to a blazing inferno!

In one night, with one lie, the world became a ticking time bomb! With more and more lies, that bomb was ready to explode! There were protests from Black Lives Matter, amongst others. There were gay pride protests and marches because Jussie said it was a hate crime! Everyone was quick to point the finger at Ola. He must be homophobic! They couldn't point at me and say the same; Jussie had made sure it appeared as if I were in a relationship with him.

Ola has no ill feelings toward anyone. Neither of us does. If I had to guess, I think Jussie was interested in me, but he knew I wasn't gay. When it came to his lies being questioned, he chose to make my brother into a villain. All anyone had to do was look my brother up on the internet. He and I, among others, were at Chicago's Pride Parade in 2015. We dressed as Trojan warriors and handed out condoms to those there.

More than one of the men there hit on me and him. When we told them we were straight, many said that was a shame and asked that we just flex a little for them. We were happy too. If either of us had an issue with the LGBTQ+, we wouldn't have done that. Not to mention we were bouncers for years in Boystown! Yet Jussie's claim of homophobia was taken as truth!

There were numerous celebrities who immediately came out in support of Jussie. From presidents to movie stars, everyone wanted to support him in this terrible time. When the truth came out, some of them deleted all support posts on their social media. Not that deleting it erased it from the internet. But after the harsh comments about the 'Osundairo brothers' or the' Nigerian brothers,' my brother and I were still the bad guys. Evidence has shown we were used as were they in this scheme Jussie had. Yet no one has shown us any form of support.

Ola: There was a picture of Jussie released from his hospital bed with Lee Danials, the man behind Empire, in the corner. It was a screenshot of Jussie while in a Facetime video. Lee Daniels was one who tweeted about the 'attack' almost immediately when the 'attack' was reported.

Lee Daniels Post (from Entertainment Tonight and ABC News):

"It's taken me a minute to come to social media about this because, Jussie, you are my son. You didn't deserve, nor anybody deserves to have a noose put around your neck, to have bleach thrown on you, to be called 'die faggot' nigger', or whatever they said to you. You are better than that. We are better than that. America is better than that. It starts at home... It starts at home, yo.

We have to love each other regardless of what sexual orientation we are because it shows that we are united on a united front. And no racist fuck can come in and do the things that they did to you," Daniels added. "Hold your head up, Jussie. I'm with you; I'll be there in a minute; it's just another fucking day in America.

Of course, there's some doubt. I'm telling you that because I love him so much," Daniels said. "That's the torture that I'm in right now because it's literally, if it were to happen to your son and your child, how would you feel? You would feel, 'Please, God, please let there be that glimmer of hope that there is some truth in this story.' That's why it's been so painful. It was a flood of pain."

I was on *Empire,* as was Bola. Yet when all this went down, and then the truth was revealed, did Lee Daniels say anything to us? Even if it had just been a 'Hate that happened to you.' But nothing. A few years before, the man had taken a picture with me on set during a break in the filming and posted it on his Instagram, and when the truth was revealed...nothing!

This picture was to show the wounds Jussie received from the 'attack.' I gave him a little noogie; that was the only mark I left on him.

When the truth came out, suddenly, things changed. The support began to pull away. They realized how they had messed up. Including Lee Daniels. This time he spoke to a magazine, *Vulture,* and said he was 'beyond embarrassed.'

But again, nothing was said to Bola or me. We know we will never get apologies from Jussie or any of the people who in some way tarnished our reputations. We're fine with that. As far as we are concerned, this book is the last we will talk about the hoax. We are so much more than that! We just want to get on with our lives. That includes auditions! We haven't had a chance to really audition for TV or movies since the fake lynching. We've had a video here and there, but that is backtracking in our acting. We had gotten up to speaking roles and the lead in a movie or two. That has all stopped now.

Bola: It is more than just getting our lives going again that concerns us. We will make that happen as it is our destiny. What we are concerned about is how actual people are victims of race crimes and hate crimes. From the day he reported the 'lynching' as real, Jussie made it so every future and the past person who files one of these types of crimes will be called into question. The officers, as well as the public, will stop and ask if it is true or a hoax. That shouldn't be an issue!

A crime against race and sexual preference should immediately be taken seriously! Not just to the police and other law enforcement, but to the people as well! We need to bring change to this world! It shouldn't matter if you are black, white, Latino, Puerto Rican, or any other race! If you want to tattoo your skin to be pink with yellow polka dots, it shouldn't matter! We are all the same when you peel away the skin! Why should anyone be made to feel inferior by the color of their skin? Are we, not all made in the Almighty's image?

Racial issues come from all races, not just black. Looking back on this 'lynching' the roles Jussie had us playing were racist. He had us being white men not just 'attacking' but trying to lynch a black man. But it was also racist in the way he had us, two black men, portray ourselves as white men. We didn't have a white face, but he wanted us to act white. Had the roles been reversed, there would have been hell to pay! In recent years, people have come under scrutiny for things they may have said or done in the past. For instance, the movie 'White Chicks.' The main characters become 'white' girls. Yet they are black men. This has been called into question as something wrong. But at the time, no one saw an issue with it. It was a funny movie. That was it.

But what Jussie asked my brother and me to do was wrong, not just to 'attack' him but want us to be 'Southern white men' attempting to put a noose around his neck while doing it. These kinds of prejudices were easy for him to latch onto because they are so common these days. As I've said, hindsight is 20/20. At the time, we were just doing the role we had been assigned.

Regardless of why we did it, we want to say we are sorry. Jussie owes you an apology as well, but you'll probably be waiting as long as we will for that!

There is so much hate in the world! Why must we find another thing to build hate on?

These issues have been an ever-increasing thing! For Jussie to have taken that fear we face on a daily basis and lie about it is like smacking anyone who is of a different race and those of a different sexual orientation in the face! He made something that is serious and happens every day into something to be questioned. A hoax that, when all was said and done, left the world wary of the next 'lynching hoax.' Will it be true? Or did someone else want their few minutes of fame by faking an 'attack;?

Ola: I have to give it to Former President Donald Trump. When word got out about it being a hoax, he once more weighed in on it.

President Donald Trump:

"In addition to great incompetence and corruption, The Smollett case in Chicago is also about a Hate Crime. Remember, "MAGA COUNTRY DID IT!" That turned out to be a total lie and had nothing to do with "MAGA COUNTRY." Serious stuff, and not even an apology to millions of people!" (Tweet May 25, 2019)

He followed up with this:

"FBI and DOJ to review the outrageous. Jussie Smollett case in Chicago. It is an embarrassment to our nation!" (Tweet March 28, 2019)

Bola: His son, Donald Trump Jr., took things further! I don't know if he was mad about the red hat and MAGA country comment or what, but he obviously felt more needed to be said. He went on *Twitter* and reminded all of us how Jussie's supporters had been quick to jump on what Jussie said happened. They had the hashtag #JusticeForJussie on post after post! When the truth came out, Trump Jr. didn't hesitate to call everyone out!

Donald Trump Jr. tweeted:

"Hey, Hollywood and media types, I've noticed a lot of you deleted your #JusticeForJussie tweets…what's the matter, don't you want Justice for him anymore?" #frauds (Tweet February 18, 2019)

Say what you may about the Trumps; at least they recognized Jussie for the liar he is! President Trump should ask Jussie why he needed this modern-day lynching.

Chapter Twenty-Seven

GOT A SECRET...CAN YOU KEEP IT?

Chicago is a place where anything can happen and usually does. Why not a modern-day lynching? There are many questions about politics and corruption within many agencies. Was it because of this, that Jussie chose to assist in this modern-day lynching? Were there people in the right places to make sure this didn't come back and bite him in the ass?

Bola: Ola and I thought our lives would return to normal. But that didn't happen. Everywhere we looked we were being whispered about or blamed it seemed. We went from having multiple casting calls a week to zero. We didn't do anything wrong, as was shown by the court case. Yet here it is years later, and we still are under that shadow! As well as Tina Glandian's comment about white face! All because we helped a friend!

Ola: For helping a friend stage a modern-day lynching. Looking back on it, Bola and I have taken note of what was going on in the United States at the time of this hoax. What reason did Jussie have for wanting to stage a modern-day lynching? What reason would anyone have for faking such a thing?

Bola: As we have tried to get our lives back on track, we have had time to really look at what was going on in the nation and possibly the true reason Jussie wanted the 'lynching hoax'.

When Jussie first showed me the threatening letter, he mentioned he wasn't happy with the attitude of the studio, and that they didn't seem to take the threat seriously. He never really told me he wanted more money or a better role. He didn't really say what he thought the studio should have done. I've been asked if I thought he wanted to make more money or get a better role on the show, but that doesn't sound like a good reason. I mean, his family is well known not to mention his many influential friends. If he wanted something like that, he wouldn't need to fake a 'lynching'. There had to be something more than money or status to put his acting and music career on the line.

Ola: As time got closer to Jussie's appeal, we knew our lives were once more going to be front and center to every media outlet and true crime fans out there. As we braced for Jussie 2.0 to hit, Bola and I began once more questioning what Jussie's possible motive could have been. One of the things I don't understand was why he was adamant the 'lynching hoax' had to be carried out on January 29th. It was just one thing after another interfering with the plan! Being stuck on the tarmac, the flight delayed, and so on. Not to mention it was in the middle of a winter vortex! No one should be out and about at two in the morning in that weather! Why couldn't we do the lynching hoax after he was back in town, on a day when we weren't freezing our asses off!

Bola: Looking back, I think it was because we were leaving town for two weeks. At the time I didn't see how crazy it was to have us do it that night. When we were in the 'planning' stage, Jussie wanted to know when we were going to Nigeria. The 'lynching hoax' had to take place before we left. He never said why, but there had to be some reason. What was Jussie's need for it to be done that night? Honestly, his lame excuse about going to Subway for a tuna sandwich and a salad was just ridiculous! If I'd been one of the police officers, he told his reason for being out at two in the morning, I would have laughed at him. Seriously! It's below freezing, you've just gotten off a plane you'd been sitting on for hours and hours and the first thing you do is go to Subway.

Ola: What possible reason would bring anyone out in that kind of cold at that time of night? Bola and I wouldn't have been there if it was our choice! If this was just a ploy to get better pay or whatever, what was the rush? That never sat right with me. But as I've said before, it was a gig, and we were paid to do our parts as we are with any acting gig.

As the appeal got underway, we revisited the many questions we had from that fateful night four years ago. It all came down to a simple question. Why? We decided to look at the bigger picture. What was going on in the U. S. at the time? I felt if we could figure out the why we would have a better idea of why Jussie insisted it happen that night! Why the rush? Why a noose? Why did the noose need to be around his neck? Why was he still wearing it nearly an hour later when the police arrived?

Bola: Everything seemed to begin after the letter was received. Was there more to this mysterious letter than what was on the surface? Was the 'lynching hoax' about something more important than a threat to Jussie's life? What if there was never any threat? What if the threat was faked because of the bigger picture? What if he wasn't the one who thought this scheme up? He has repeatedly said he didn't plan the 'lynching hoax'. What if he didn't? Was he instructed by the directors or producers in this *'movie'* we were all a part of to send the letter?

Ola: It seems the letter is a means to an end. It was the first 'threat' and was built on from there. But by who and why? If we knew who had sent the letter, the actual proof of who it was, things would make more sense.

Bola: The last I heard; the FBI hadn't been able to find out the origin of the letter. Did Jussie send it with the powdery substance as act one in this movie? Was Jussie made aware of a need for a modern-day lynching? But why would there be a need for such a thing? And why would a black man, gay or not, want to perpetrate a 'lynching hoax'?

Ola: Jussie insisted we have a red hat and a rope to make a noose out of. As I have said, I didn't know how to make a noose. What black man would? If I hadn't been able to find a video on YouTube it wouldn't have happened. Hell, all that was missing was a tree!

Bola: Do you know the kind of mindset that takes? I don't know a single black man who would willingly put a noose around their neck! Not ONE!

Ola: Exactly! Who in their right mind would come up with such a horrendous plan as to have two people fake 'lynch' you? No man would come up with such a plan, much less a black man! There is never a reason for a black man to even joke about a lynching, fake or not!

Bola: There has to be a reason Jussie would do this. He was on a number-one-rated show and had a burgeoning music career. He was fast becoming a star in both fields. Why did he want anything else? Look at where he is now.

Ola: Could there be a political angle to the 'fake lynching'? Jussie needed us to say this was MAGA country and wear a red hat! We were supposed to get a MAGA hat but if we couldn't find one, just get a red hat. He was insistent we give off the impression we were Southern white men. What was so important we had to use the president's slogan in a fake lynching? That never made any sense. Why did it have anything to do with politics? With the election year near, the candidates had already thrown their hats in the ring. Did Jussie choose what we said or was someone else providing the script?

Bola: I keep coming back to Jussie putting the noose on himself and leaving it on for almost an hour! He waited until the police came and mentioned he was wearing it so they could see it before he removed it. There is no way I would have willingly put a noose around my neck, much less wear it for that long! The man I was friends with, never gave off the impression he would do any of this. That's why I didn't take him seriously when he first mentioned it.

Could it be that Jussie was a pawn in a bigger game? Were the directors and producers looking for a well-known face that checked all the boxes? Black, check. Gay, check. Was he told he wouldn't get into any trouble? Jussie never mentioned the police being involved when we discussed the 'lynching hoax'.

Ola: The hoax was meant to be for social media, according to Jussie. That was why I was shocked to find it on Twitter and on the news. Even if Jussie did check all the boxes, that still doesn't explain why he would do such a thing. He had everything, why risk it? Could Jussie have been promised he would be protected? With different degrees of the 'lynching hoax' were there different producers on each of those stages as well? Did Jussie know the directors and producers and believed they would protect him from being written off?

If there was a need for a modern-day lynching, a young gay black man would be the perfect person to use. But if you were agreeable to doing such a thing, what guarantees would you have that your life would be unchanged or better than it had been?

Bola: Maybe he thought he would have a legacy to leave behind more than his acting and music career. There could be a historical aspect that made the 'modern-day lynching hoax' worth it.

Ola: It was with that thought, we turned our attention to a possible motive for Jussie's plan. There was an anti-lynching bill that has been before Congress over 200 times. Each time the bill is altered in some way or given a new name.

Bola: This bill was pitched to the Senate in December of 2018. The Senate passed it, but the House didn't even look at it. This bill dies once again.

January 29, 2019, Jussie arranged a modern-day lynching. Over the next few days, there were numerous supportive Tweets on Twitter for Jussie, from prominent individuals mentioning a modern-day lynching.

Ola: Sixteen days later, the anti-lynching bill is back before Congress. The senators presenting the bill have altered the wording a little and changed the name. When pitching the bill, the senators referenced a young black man who had recently been almost lynched. The Senate passed it immediately. The House passed it, except for a hold-out vote. One of the senators thought the dialogue of the bill needed a little clarification. Later the final re-write of the bill was named The Emmett Till Bill. In 1955, Emmett Till was the last known man to be lynched.

Bola: Could this be the reason Jussie needed a modern-day lynching hoax? He insisted it be done that night, regardless of all the delays and the below-freezing temperature, because we were leaving the next day for two weeks. The bill was coming up for a vote during the time we would be in Nigeria.

Ola: A noose was required. A noose that Jussie put on himself and wore for almost an hour.

Bola: I've been thinking about how Jussie behaved after his guilty verdict. He repeatedly stated he was not suicidal. Why would he say that over and over? That always seemed odd to me. Was he afraid for his life? It's not like high-profile inmates haven't been found with a noose around their lifeless body. I can't help wondering if it has something to do with his reason for doing the lynching hoax.

Ola: I doubt we will ever know the reason Jussie needed this. Whatever it was, it has become a part of history. He will forever be known as the person who hired two friends to fake a modern-day lynching. And we will forever be known as the two friends who helped him.

Bola: We always knew we would be known after we were gone, but I never imagined that this would be a part of why I was remembered!

Ola: It's how we are remembered in this modern-day lynching hoax that I don't like. It has made me more cautious when agreeing to help someone.

Bola: If this were the reason, Jussie needed my help, he could have told me. I can't say I would definitely have helped him, but I would have thought it over. Whatever the reason, Jussie, Ola, and I are going to be remembered in this historic event.

At the time, Vice President Kamala Harris was a senator.

A Senator who was trying to get an anti-lynching bill passed. When word of Jussie's hoax got out, she tweeted this:

> "@JussieSmollett is one of the kindest, most gentle human beings I know. I'm praying for his quick recovery. This was an attempted modern-day lynching. No one should have to fear for their life because of their sexuality or color of their skin. We must confront this hate."

Fellow Senator and anti-lynching bill sponsor, Cory Booker, tweeted:

> "The vicious attack to own actor, Jussie Smollett was an attempted modern-day lynching. I'm glad he's safe. To those in Congress who don't feel the urgency to pass our Anti-Lynching bill designating lynching as a federal hate crime-I urge you to pay attention. Ebony.com/news/Jussie-sm…"

Joy-Ann (Pro-Democracy) Reid tweeted:

> "Nooses never really disappeared as messages of a very specific kind of terror, but every time they're used, my God, it's chilling. Praying for Jussie's full recovery. And for all of us."

Joy-Ann was responding to this tweet by NBC News on January 29th, 2019.

> "Police: "Empire" actor Jussie Smollett was assaulted in Chicago on Tuesday by two men who hurled racial and homophobic slurs at him and wrapped a rope around his neck, the actor has told police; the incident is being investigated as a hate crime. Nbcnews.2DGM1dv"

Chapter Twenty-Eight

WHERE WERE WE, MR. PRESIDENT?

Ola: Fox News invited us to the president's White House Correspondents Dinner. This was a shock to us.

Bola: A shock but also a great opportunity! Of course, we went! There was something ironic about us being there.

Ola: Ah, yes, they had condemned my brother and me through their public support of Jussie, and now we're having dinner!

Bola: The President and Vice President tweeted their support for Jussie after the 'attack' but didn't acknowledge how my brother and I were done.

> **Biden tweeted**: "What happened today to @Jussie Smollett must never be tolerated in this country. We must stand up and demand that we no longer give this hate safe harbor and that homophobia and racism have no place on our streets or in our hearts. We are with you, Jussie."
>
> **Kamala Harris**: "@Jussie Smollett is one of the kindest, most gentle human beings I know. I'm praying for his quick recovery..."

Ola: We weren't expecting anything when we went to this dinner. We met Senator Amy Klobuchar, among a few celebrities such as Winnie Harlow, Kyle Kuzma.

Bola: We were recognized, but no one shunned us. There were whispers throughout the dinner hall. 'There goes the Osundairo brothers.' It wasn't said in a bad way. We felt welcomed. This is one of those moments you can't really believe even though you are there. We were sitting amongst prominent people.

Ola: It was very surreal. Out of all the moments I have done in my life at this point, I would say this ranks up toward the top.

Bola: Definitely ranks in my top ten! It was a night of fun and excitement. We didn't meet the President or Vice President, but we met many others. My brother and I got to experience something many wish to do but never get the opportunity. This is one of the things I will never forget.

Ola: Jussie caused Bola and me to miss out on so many acting opportunities. I would never have thought when our lives were tarnished by his actions, that we would end up rubbing elbows with politicians and celebrities.

Bola: Ola and I are grateful for the opportunity. Thank you, Fox News for inviting us.

Chapter Twenty-Nine

WE THANK YOU

Ola: First and foremost, Bola and I want to thank our Heavenly Father. It is through Him we met those who would help us to clear our names. He has always been with us. We are forever thankful for His presence in our lives.

Bola: We want to thank our family, here and in Nigeria. They were there through all of the lies and truth coming out. Thank you all for your support and love.

Ola: When the case against Jussie was dropped, the records were sealed. We never thought to see them. To find out why he was released without a slap on the hand!

The next thing we knew, Circuit Judge Steven Watkins said the sealing was reversed! The files were available to be gone through. Shortly after that, we heard a retired judge, Sheila O'Brien, had gone through the entire case and decided justice hadn't been served. She was the one who petitioned for a special prosecutor to look at it. It was because of this woman justice would be done!

Judge O'Brien, we can never thank you enough for helping us clear our name. The Osundairo name is one of royalty. Our name is one we are proud of. Because of my desire to help a friend, that name was tarnished, not because of what we did, but because the person who had us make the 'attack' chose to make it so.

If not for your taking the time to read over the trial transcript, we may not have had our day in court. We can never fully thank you for the justice you have done us. We will forever be grateful that you took the time out of your retirement to see justice done.

Bola: We also want to show our appreciation for Special Prosecutor Mr. Webb, Sean Wieber, Sam Mendenhall, and the rest of the team. You believed us when you heard our story. You worked with us to get us ready for court. We can be a little headstrong at times, but you and your team kept us straight. Thank you for helping us get justice.

A very big thank you goes to our lawyer, and friend, Gloria Schmidt Rodriguez, for answering and listening to a voicemail in the early morning hours from a woman she had given her card to many months before. Thank you for hearing our story and wanting to see the truth revealed. We couldn't have done any of this without you there!

We have worked many hours and countless days to get this hoax exposed. You stood by our side from day one and have been there ever since. You will never know how blessed we feel to have you in our lives. The Almighty knew we needed someone ferocious to get us through this. You may be small, but you are the lion we needed! You are more than our lawyer and friend. You are family!

Ola: Chicago Police Department has a reputation for being hard asses. There have been many issues that have given the CPD a tarnished reputation. Even so, they didn't treat my brother and me badly. From the beginning, they were friendly. They didn't give us answers when we asked, but we didn't give them to them either.

We found out that after we were released, the police department was worried when we refused to eat or drink anything. If Gloria hadn't gotten there when she did, they were planning to take us to the hospital.

Our culture doesn't like to deal with the police for many reasons. When all this went down, that was one thing I told myself. But in fairness, CPD treated us better than I expected they would. I can't say if it is because they already suspected the 'attack' was fake or if they were just a few of the good detectives in CPD. Whatever it was, my brother and I want to express our gratitude for them taking the time to hear us out and then see that justice was done. It wasn't their fault the first charges were dismissed.

Bola: Those people who have helped us with the docuseries and podcast have our gratitude. They took two brothers and showed the world we weren't the people we were portrayed to be. Scott Eldridge from Pilgrim Media and Lionsgate Sound, Ola, and I thank you from the bottom of our hearts. We had no idea how the docuseries or podcast would turn out, but you coached us and made the process painless. Thank you!

Ola: Though we are just beginning the process of publishing our story, Bola and I want to thank Tammy Corwin and the Words Mater Publishing team for all their help!

Because of Lionsgate, Pilgrim Media, and Words Matter Publishing, we have been given a chance to get what really happened out there, not just in a docuseries and a podcast but a book as well. Through these publications, we have been able to expose the truth completely for the viewers/readers/listeners.

Bola: There were numerous people behind the scenes with each of these people that assisted in the outcome we have. We can't thank you all individually, even though we would try, but we want you to know how thankful we are to have had you in our corner.

Through all of this, Ola and I have been guided in the direction the Almighty wants us to go. He led us to each of these people, in one way or another, to see that the truth was revealed.

Bola in tribal dress.

Bola and Ola at Chicago Pride 2015

Bola and Ola

Bola with a friend.

Chapter Thirty

LIFE GOES ON

Ola: That part of our life is thankfully over! Time to get our lives and careers back on track. I know we won't ever be able to completely wipe out things. It would be nice if one day people said, 'Jussie who?'

Bola: Moving on with our lives, Ola and I go to a training camp in Florida where I train with ex-world champion Keith Thurman. He teaches us a lot of valuable knowledge and experiences. We are concentrating on getting my professional boxing career going. Ola is training to box as well.

In May 2021, I was supposed to fight in Dubai. This is to be my first professional fight. I'm ready, and then the President of Dubai dies. The fight gets canceled. We searched for another fight and found one on June 18th in Rosemont, IL. This was now my first professional fight, and I won.

I have only been boxing for a few years, and already I am #1 in the US and was on the Olympic Boxing Team! This is unheard of for someone young as me to have gotten this far so quickly!

Ola: I am training with Bola, but I am also working as the promoter. The way a fight works is there has to be a promoter, someone that throws or hosts a fight. Usually, there's a side A and a side B concerning fighters. The A-side, a lot of the time, is assigned to the promoter. The B side is an opponent that they get from anywhere to come to fight the A side, the promoter's fighter.

Bola: I'm not signed with a promoter, nor do I have a manager. A lot of the fights that I've been doing, I've been on the B side, which is very risky. Especially if you're good because it's risky in the sense that if you don't knock your opponent out, they can cheat you. They can rob you in the fight, so it's very risky to be on the B side.

The first fight I had was a 50/50 fight, even though the guy was 3-0 as a professional. He had three wins, zero losses. I was coming in with no wins, no losses. The guy so happened not to be signed with the promoter. The promoter actually wanted to sign me. He let me fight on his card, but I didn't eventually end up signing with him. In the second fight, I was on the B-side. The third on the A-side, but I wasn't signed with the promoter.

What happens is a promoter can throw a fight. And he could be selling slots on his card or in his show. Selling slots means you have to pay, let's say $500 slot fee. After the $500.00, you have to pay for your opponent, which I did. So, I had to pay $1700 for my third fight–$500 for the slot fee and then $1200 to my opponent. That's how boxing works.

My fourth fight was in Los Angles, California. I came in on the B side. When you're on the B-side, you're coming in to lose. They expect you to lose. I was 3-0 fighting someone that was 9-1. I was brought in to lose. I didn't. I knocked my guy out in the sixth round. They were mad as hell about that. Because they obviously invested money in the other guy on the A-side. I knew I could beat him because I had watched some of his videos and I studied him. I could beat this guy, so I accepted the fight.

Usually, in the boxing world, we have an advisor. I have two advisors, Tony Simpson, and Fres Oquendo, that help me look for fights, so he'll call different promoters, and then the promoters would tell him that they have a fight available, but they'll link him with someone else that has a fight available, and then we'd see if we want to take the fight. Also, there's a group on Facebook where people go for promoters and match-makers. Type in fights that they have coming up, and they're looking to match certain people.

I'm on that website. My brother usually goes on there, and then he submits me for different fights. If they want the fight, they'll take it. Often opponents won't take the fight. Once they see my picture, they are too scared, or they'll think it's too risky for them to take the fight.

I've had matches where I was supposed to go fight someone on ESPN. Then at the last minute, they refused the fight because they didn't want to fight me, even though they had a better record. They've been boxing longer and weren't willing to take the risk.

Fighting is more than just money. How you rank helps get you more fights; sometimes, I am making nothing off the fight except the ranking. In my third fight, I wasn't signed to the promoter. I had to buy the slot. I had to pay for my opponent. I don't get a purse; my opponent does, $1200. When you're signed with a promoter, you usually get a purse every time.

I'm independent right now. When you're independent, you buy a slot fee, and you're paying for your opponent. You don't get a purse unless I go on the B-side like how I did when I went to Cali. I went on the B side, and I got paid. In my last fight in Mexico, I had to pay for my flight out there as well as the opponent and the slot.

In Nigeria, as well as in Mexico, I had to pay about $6500 to fight my opponent. I had to pay for my flight out there, pay the opponent, and pay the sanction fee. Once again, I was without a coach in my corner. It was easier to find someone as I was in Nigeria and had been there before for the African Games. I went to the same coach, but he wasn't very good at wrapping my hands. They were wrapped pretty tight, which was hurting my hands, but it was already game time. There was no time to do anything about it. I had a little anxiety during the preparation leading up to the fight.

While I was sparring with one of my opponents, while in Nigeria, his coach was busy watching what I was doing. He had picked up on some of what I was doing when we were sparing and was giving that information to his fighter. Supposedly, the coach didn't know that I would be fighting his fighter when we were sparing. He had an advantage, not that it mattered. I decided to not knock out. I won the majority decision in the twelfth round. I am #1 in Africa. In Nigeria, I was fighting for a belt. I was there for the African Continental. I won. I'm ranked number one in Africa and #25 in the world, with only five fights at the time.

I saw the money as an investment in me. Thus far, I have paid more than I have won, but I see it as an investment. With the route I am going, we don't want me to sign with a manager. A manager looks at the position. They see all that is going on with us at the moment, the docuseries, the podcast, and the book. I don't want someone to come in and reap off of things that they didn't help me get.

A few we have talked to want a certain percentage of my likeness and image. I said hell no! They want to do merchandise and all this stuff to make money. They want control over me. If I were a kid, I might fall for it, but I know how the game works. I'm not giving anyone the right to my face or name.

Ola: I am doing all the background stuff for my brother. I'm the administrator. I go over the promotors and managers reaching out and helping Bola pick his fights. I talk to a lot of matchmakers and try to help. This leaves Bola to focus on training and fighting for the most part.

I have started boxing recently and am training to be in matches too. There are influencers that throw fights. I'm looking to get into one of them possibly. In the meantime, I am training and getting my skills where they need to be.

I guess you could say I am Bola's manager and his promoter. I have been in his corner a few times, like the one he did in California. Bola has Nate Jones and Jeff Mason in his corner most of the time. Nate was Mayweather's former coach. Jeff Mason also has a bronze medal in the Olympics, like Nate. Jeff was also a pro fighter back in the day.

At this point, neither of us are making much in the way of money. I do the occasional meal and workout plan. I also train a few times a week. It is cheaper to fight in Mexico. Bola will take a fight or two down there ever so often, but he usually doesn't make much. Boxing is a sport that you have to have patience with. If you're looking for a big payday, boxing isn't it. Not to begin with. First, you have to build a name and reputation for yourself. That is what my brother is doing.

Bola: We are also working on NFTs–Non-Fungible Tokens. It has to do with cryptocurrency. Ola and I have a song we did together called

Magic that can be found on Spotify and Apple Music. It's by the Nigerian Brothers. Ola and I have been cast in a couple of videos since the Jussie debacle. Our lives are going where they were always meant to go.

My life is on track to become the person I always knew I would be. I look at boxing as a vehicle to get me there. My goal is to become an undisputed World Champion. I want to hold the main belts of the four sanctioning bodies. God willing, this will happen by the time I am thirty-five. I don't want to be in boxing too long. I understand the dangers that come with boxing and getting your head repeatedly hit. The trauma that it can cause could result in permanent damage. I would like to be seen as the people's champ. I enjoy athletic challenges. I wouldn't mind doing other sports and making my way to the top of them as well.

I want to continue acting and see where that leads. Following in my family's footsteps in Nigeria, I will go into politics. I want to unite West Africa and make one economy. To blend all cultures and ethnic groups into a united West Africa, Africa in general, but mainly focusing on West Africa. There's beauty in having differences in diversity. With my brother's help, we will find a way to make that work. So that's my goal in life.

I went on a boxing tour in 2021 across Africa. I called out for lawmakers and leaders to allocate more recesses and resources for underprivileged talents in West Africa for sports, fitness, and arts. I was quoted in an interview saying, "With time, training, dedication, and investment to produce results, Africa can be great again. Let's break the odds and make a remarkable representation on the global stage. The music and entertainment industry is already making evident global progress. The time is now." This is just one of the things I want to do.

I think it's very important that our people get the resources they need. There's a lot of talent in Africa, particularly Nigeria, with over two hundred million people. There's a lot of talent there but not a lot of resources. So, I called on the politicians, the lawmakers, to give more money to the youth. There are a lot of us that can use our talent and make better use of ourselves, but we just need those opportunities. So that's why I did that. I went on the news and made a statement. I was on tour from winning the championship and felt that would give those in charge a moment to stop and think.

Lawmakers can't make changes in the blink of an eye; I know that. It is a work in progress that I will hopefully set in motion. This is one of the things I plan to do when I am in politics in Nigeria. This, amongst other things, education and healthcare are important in uniting Africa.

I have been boxing for four years and I am a US Champion.

Ola: I've only been boxing for five months. Unlike my brother, I'm not looking to be a world champion. That isn't my goal. I just want a vehicle to showcase my talent in sports as well as acting. Once I have accomplished that, I will join my brother in uniting West Africa. Together we will turn West Africa into a united culture.

Bola and I do calisthenics. It's for tightening the core. It exercises your large muscle groups. You have to really be into fitness to get into calisthenics. We have been known to stop at a stop sign, and one of us gets out and makes this one move where we use all our arm strength to hold our body as we stretch out vertically to the sign. One of our favorite moves is where we put our heads together, then clutch each other's shoulders and raise our bodies and legs off the floor. This move pulls on our core muscles, our abs. We look like we are doing a large V. You have to trust yourself and your partner if you attempt to do anything like that.

Bola: We've seen some of the memes of us; we've even made a few ourselves about the incident. We aren't trying to make it into a comical event, but in a way, it is funny. Life is too hard to take everything so seriously. Jussie's entire plan is crazy to the point it is comical. Looking back on it, we can see that. Now is it one big joke? I don't think of it like that. It is just something that was blown way out of proportion. And unfortunately, it will continue to do so. The internet will see to that.

There have been a lot of questions we've been asked over the years as well as those that no one wants to ask directly but just puts on social media, I guess in the hopes someone will ask us for them or that someone who knows nothing about us will make up lies to. We are going to take this time to answer some of them.

One of the most asked ones is If I would have believed Jussie or the 'attackers' had I been an innocent bystander. Suppose I would have believed the lie. In other words, if someone else had 'attacked' him, would I have believed the evidence or Jussie's performance? Let's be honest; that's what it was, a performance. The same as it was for us.

But getting back to the question, would I believe his lies? Yes. Jussie is a great actor. I believe he put on an Oscar-worthy performance from the day he asked my brother and me to do the fake 'attack.' I can see why it is hard for some people to take our word for it. We aren't asking that they do. We asked that they believed the evidence.

Ola: Jussie and I were more acquaintances than friends. Does that mean I wouldn't have bought his lies as the truth if Bola and I weren't involved in any way? Yes. It was a great performance. Truly he did an amazing job, right down to the tears he shed when talking about wanting a little gay boy to know he doesn't have to hide. If I had been an outsider looking in going solely off his acting, not the evidence, I'd have believed him. Dude's that good!

Bola: Do I think Jussie truly saw me as a friend, a brother? I think he did. Obviously, I didn't know him as well as I thought I did. But I do believe he saw me as a friend, someone he could trust. I think that is why he asked me to do this 'attack' instead of anyone else. He knew he could trust me, and because I was a boxer, I could pull my punch and still make him look good.

There are still the occasional trolls popping up now and then on our social media. Those that believe it was true regardless of what the courts have proven. Some of these people wouldn't believe it was a hoax if Jussie did finally admit it! That's how some of his fans are, but that doesn't bother us. We know the truth, as does America. Whether they believe it is up to them.

If they want to post negative stuff on our social media, go ahead. We will delete it. We won't get into a pissing match with any of them. That's what trolls want. They want to upset your day so that they can go back and forth with you. It's a waste of time and energy. If they want to have a pissing match with our supporters, that is up to them. But know this;

these trolls are free to do what they want. In the end, it is them who are in the wrong.

The Almighty has given us the ability to forgive those around us. That includes these people who troll the internet just to make someone feel worse than them. That includes Jussie. I choose to forgive these trolls. I choose to forgive Jussie.

Ola: If I were to see Jussie one day, I would wait to see how he responds. If he chooses to ignore me and walk on by, that's fine. I will continue on my way. I would probably say hi as it would be the polite thing to do.

Bola: I have no problem saying what's up to him. How he chooses to respond is a reflection of him. I will be cordial. I won't let any negativity bring me down to that level again.

I don't think Jussie could have found anyone else to do this if he had tried. I only agreed because I felt indebted to him and saw it as helping a friend out. Of the friends of Jussie's I met over the time we hung out, I can't think of a single one who would have agreed to this, in my opinion. I am one of those friends who will help in any way I can. Friends of mine throughout my life can attest to that.

When this all played out on the global stage, not a single friend of mine from any time in my life believed I would do such a thing. Not a single friend initially came out and asked how could I do such a thing. Many friends questioned us about the incident after Tina Glandian's white face comment. Those I heard from told me they knew it was a lie. My brother and I weren't the type to attack someone. That is one reason Ola, and I wanted to do this book. We've done the docuseries and the podcast, which are great. But a book is something you can hold in your hands and read about us, about the truth. My brother and I are good people. This incident has taken our lives and turned them upside down.

We were on our way up in our acting career. We had multiple roles with more to come. We were signed to the hardest talent agency to get in with, Grace Talent Agency. This is one of the top-rated talent agencies in Chicago. Once this hoax was brought to light, suddenly, we weren't the kind of clients they wanted. I can't say for sure, but if I had to guess, over the last few years, I have lost roles that would have brought me more than $200,000, most likely more.

Ola: A friend of ours hooked us up with someone at Pilgrim Media, the part of Lionsgate that does unscripted shows. They wanted to do a docuseries on the hoax. They also wanted to have us on a podcast.

Bola: Pilgrim Media has been great to us. Finally, being able to tell what happened, to clear up the lies and the accusations, has been a relief! We reenacted the 'attack' and answered some questions about why we used bleach or why a hot sauce bottle.

Ola: The podcast gave us a chance to answer more questions one on one. It also gave us a chance to introduce ourselves more or less to the public. Us, not the 'attackers' or 'suspected attackers,' us, Bola, and Ola Osundairo.

They were so welcoming; Charlie Webster was a great host. Working with everyone from Pilgrim Media and Lionsgate has been great! We have been treated with respect at every turn, not just by the amazing people at Lionsgate and Pilgrim Media but by the public as well. Overall, the tweets we've seen since the docuseries and podcast have been favorable. A lot of people out there support us and want to see where we go from here.

Bola: Going back over everything first with the docuseries and again with the podcast, we realized there were some major holes in Jussie's plan. At the time, we didn't see it because it wasn't our plan. It was a gig, a gig to help a friend. Looking back at the incident now as we write this book, there are so many holes in the plan that if I'd had more time, I would have seen. Jussie planned the entire hoax and only gave Ola and me two days before he wanted it to happen. We barely had time to figure out all the ins and outs of what Jussie was asking. At the time, I was seeing this as an acting gig a friend asked me to help with.

When Jussie pointed out the camera that was supposed to catch everything, not once did I think to ask him how he would be getting the footage from it. I didn't ask him if he knew the camera was facing the way he needed it to. This is something I should have asked, but in my mind, I saw it as an acting gig, and my script didn't include any of the behind-the-scenes stuff.

Another thing I should have thought of at the time was why would Jussie be out at that time of night to grab a sub and salad at *Subway?* He just flew in from New York, and it was in the middle of a polar vortex. Why would he go out in weather that was cold enough to freeze balls? I don't care how hungry you might be; you wouldn't go out in that kind of weather if you could afford to have someone deliver it to you! Hell, even if you didn't have anyone to deliver it!

Seriously who would have believed his story with those things in play? What did his manager think when he left him at Jussie's apartment to run down the street to grab a sub and a salad? The man didn't think it was odd. He didn't question Jussie about why he had to do it instead of having someone deliver it. Jussie could afford to pay for his own private delivery service if he wanted. Not only that, but the manager could also have picked it up, as Jussie was a star. But then Jussie wouldn't have been there for his plan to work. No Jussie, no fake attack.

Ola: It wasn't just about Jussie's holes in his part of the hoax that we should have questioned; it was what he had us do too. As Bola mentioned, it was a polar vortex. It was minus twenty! That is cold enough to freeze you to your bones! We were bundled up, and we still froze! No one would be out at that hour in that kind of cold unless it was an emergency! I'm talking life or death kind of emergency. Definitely not to get a sub!

Why would two men, be they white, southern, black, or whatever, be out in that kind of weather carrying a rope and a bottle of hot sauce with bleach in it? Why would anyone be out carrying those things at any time? This was another thing we should have seen beforehand, but it wasn't something we questioned because it was part of the script.

Bola: When looking back on everything, it's easy to see there were things we should have questioned Jussie about when he told us the plan. I think the reason we didn't, or at least I didn't, is because I was shocked when he asked. When I got over my shock, it was just another gig. I guess we didn't think about it because it wasn't our plan. We just took for granted Jussie had all these little things figured out. We did our parts, and then we put that gig behind us and went to Nigeria.

I can't help thinking some of these things we didn't think about until after is what made the police think Jussie was lying. They would have picked up on the weird parts of the script and then added Jussie wearing the noose for an hour, and his refusal to hand over his phone together and come up with Jussie planned the entire thing. It was a hoax!

Bola: Another thing that is odd is Jussie still had the sub and salad when he got home. You're supposed to have been attacked, and you still have the sense of mind to pick yourself up off the ground and your food before going home. That is crazy! You've just been 'beaten,' and you still remember to grab the food before you head home.

Ola: This book is important to us. So many people have said things about the Osundairo brothers, but not one of them knows the real us. We hope this book will show that people can make mistakes regardless of the reason the mistake was made and that you can overcome whatever that mistake is. I don't see helping my brother help a friend as a mistake. Helping a friend is always a good thing. Unfortunately, this 'friend' used him, used us in some agenda that we still don't know about.

A book is more intimate than a podcast or a docuseries. This is something you can hold in your hand. We want everyone to see we are humans, Americans, Nigerians, brothers, boxers, and friends. Our story is so much more than one incident. We are bigger than Jussie Smollett. He is but one moment in our lives. With this book, we are ending this part of our lives. This is the end of Jussie Smollett in our lives.

Bola: A friend asked me how I felt about losing the friendship Jussie, and I had. If this hadn't happened, would Jussie and I still be hanging out? I think Jussie and I would still be friends. I can't say for sure, but we probably would be. I guess it would depend on where I was in my life. He may have been but one moment in my destiny.

I was destined to meet Jussie. We were destined to become friends, brothers. When he needed someone, he came to me because it was his destiny to help me get to my destiny. My brother and I are big on faith and God. God has a mysterious way of working it all out.

Ola: Destiny is a big thing with us. I truly believe everything happens for a reason. There is a destiny you are meant to reach. You just have to take steps to get there. This that happened with Jussie was a part of my destiny. I was destined to agree to this crazy scheme. All we have gone through because of this; is a part of the destiny we are meant for. Our story is just a fourth of the way through; it is still being written. We could choose to hide somewhere until it's over or live each moment in His glory. I choose to live!

The Almighty guided us to so many people in our lives at just the right time. When we began talking about doing a book, we reached out to Gloria for suggestions. Gloria was led by someone from Pilgrim Media who knew the perfect publisher for us.

The Almighty knew we wouldn't trust just anyone with our story. We are not only doing this book, but we are also doing a children's book series on us. We want to show children they can come from all different kinds of backgrounds and still find their destiny. The children's books will also be a way to teach children about boxing. This is something we want to do as well as get them time in the gym and help them to reach their fullest potential.

Recently someone asked me what I learned from the Jussie incident and how it affected my life. I think it opened my eyes to a lot of things about how the world works on a bigger scale. I've been introduced to a lot of new experiences, some I could have done without. But each experience has made me the man I am today. I have found I can face adversity head-on and still come through it with my faith and dignity intact! I could be bitter about it, but if I were, I didn't learn the lesson I had to learn.

Bola: I was asked the same thing. I helped a friend, and in doing so, my life and my brothers became a disaster. I know that my relationship with my brother as well as with God has gotten stronger from this. I learn from every experience I have. Be it a good experience or a bad one. I take what I learn and implement it into my daily life and continue to live my life the way it is meant to be lived. I could be bitter and continually go back to that time and let it undermine me and make me into a man I wouldn't want to hang around with, let alone be. But life is too short for that.

We are from royalty. We are princes. A tilted head can't hold a crown.

www.ingramcontent.com/pod-product-compliance
Lightning Source LLC
Jackson TN
JSHW010042070125
76604JS00003B/4